The Holland Method

Workbook

James Trone

Dawnos Publishing

Contents

How to Use This Workbook

This workbook is designed as a companion to *The Holland Method* book and its accompanying teachings and video sessions, available through The Holland Method website. It's not meant to overwhelm you with information. It's meant to provide a path and practice—in presence, awareness, emotional capacity, thoughtful clarity, and self-return. **This workbook is divided into 12 modules, ideally done every day, one module per week.** A minimum of 30 minutes is required, but ideally plan for an hour first thing in the morning.

In the videos and book, we talk about the rhythm of doing The Work: small, consistent, daily practices that reorient your patterns and return you to your Larger Self. *This workbook is the place where that rhythm becomes real.* A Daily Rhythm, every day follows the same structure because repetition is what rewires the nervous system, softens the ego, and opens the pathway to the deeper self. This rhythm mirrors what you experience in the modules of the book and videos series:

Awareness → Presence → Vision → Action → Integration

Think of this workbook as your **mental health training plan**—just as you would train your body with consistent exercise, you're training your inner system to return to truth, presence, and the Larger Self.

How Each Section Works

1. Daily Reading — Reorient to Reality

Each day begins with a short reading drawn from the core ideas of The Holland Method. Remember you are not your looping thoughts. The mind creates a "virtual reality" based on past data. Self-abandonment happens when you leave the present moment. You can return through breath, body, and awareness. The good news is that the Larger Self is always available. The readings reorient you. This is your *daily calibration*, stepping out of the ego's movie reel and back into what is real. These readings are like spiritual anchors, reminding you of the truth you're learning to live from.

2. Journaling — Awareness then Understanding and then Change

Just like in the book and video sessions, awareness always precedes understanding and then change. Use the prompts to explore: What am I believing right now? What am I feeling in my body? What story is the ego running today? What would Love say? How can I reparent myself here? This isn't about getting it "right." It's *about being honest*. Journaling builds the foundation for integration—your inner connection, your clarity, your capacity to see what's actually happening instead of what fear says is happening. **Pro tip:** If you feel resistance to writing, that's often a sign something important wants to surface. Write through it.

3. Vision — Anchor Your Direction

In the book and videos, we talk about how vision is not fantasy—it's alignment with your Larger Self. Here, you reconnect to: Who you are becoming? What wants to emerge today? What small structure or action supports the vision? *Vision gives your day a north star.* It reminds you why you're doing this work when the old patterns try to pull you back. At the top of your Daily Check-In sheet, you'll see space for your vision. Keep it visible. Return to it. Let it shape how you move through your day—not your tasks dictating your energy, but your vision guiding your tasks.

4. Meditation — Return to Presence

The meditations regulate the nervous system by interrupting and integrating the fear-based mind. They shift identity from the smaller self to the Larger Self, soften and open the body, and make room for Source to meet you. This section is where you practice presence rather than just think about it. In truth, so much of The Holland Method centers around these meditative practices. If you're new to meditation, start with 5-10 minutes. If you're experienced, go deeper. The key is consistency, not duration. Remember: Stillness prepares you to receive. You're not trying to manufacture insight, you're creating space for it to arise.

Note: Please go to the Appendix: Practices Section. All guided meditations referenced in this workbook are explained with links available on Spotify, Apple Music, Amazon Music, or directly from www.hollandmethod.co You can access them anytime you need support in returning to presence.

5. Affirmation — Reprogramming to the Inner Voice

The <u>morning affirmation</u> sets your intention. The <u>evening affirmation</u> integrates your day. This echoes what we teach about thought work: You learn to speak from the Larger Self instead of the fearful imagination. Your affirmations should be: Present tense ("I am..." not "I will be...") Rooted in truth (not fake positivity, but essence). Aligned with your vision. Examples: "I can trust myself." "I am supported." "I am guided." Speak them aloud if possible. Let your body hear your voice speaking truth.

Note: Please go to the Appendix: Practices Section providing a list of affirmations.

6. Pausing — The Real Work Happens Here

In the videos, we emphasize pausing as the *"micro-practice"* that changes everything. The invitation is to set four pause points (alarms)—morning, midday, afternoon, and evening—and, when the alarm rings, simply stop and notice (Where am I? What am I feeling? What story am I believing?), take three deep breaths, and return to presence, to the body, and to truth. This small rhythm interrupts autopilot and brings unconscious patterns into awareness. It's how you practice stillness in real time—not just on a cushion, but in the middle of your actual life. It's how you catch the ego before it spirals, how you create space between stimulus and response. Most people skip this. Don't. This is where change actually happens. And each time you pause, remember your vision.

7. Physical Movement — Back to the Body

Your healing is not just cognitive. It is somatic. Movement reconnects you to the body—which, as we teach in the book and videos, is your anchor to reality. The body holds what the mind tries to avoid. When you move, you release stored emotion, reset your nervous system, and return to presence. Choose whatever helps you return: Walking, Yoga, Running, Weightlifting, Stretching, Pilates, Jiu Jitsu or other movements. Let your body lead you back to presence. You don't need an hour at the gym. Even 10-15 minutes of intentional movement shifts your state.

8. Resistance — Practice Taking Empowered Action

Resistance is often a doorway. What you have been avoiding, whether it is that creative project, that difficult conversation, or that boundary you need to set, is where your growth lives. Each day, choose one action in each domain: Creative (What wants to be expressed?) Professional (What moves your work forward?) Relationships (What connection needs attention?) Self (What does your soul need today?) These tasks build capacity, discipline, and momentum—the "muscle" of self-leadership.

Important: These aren't your regular to-do list. These are the things the smaller self resists because they require you to show up as the Larger Self. Start small. One metaphorical push-up of courage per task. That's how you build the life your soul is calling you toward.

9. Evening Review — Integrate the Day

Reflect gently: Where did I return to presence today? Where did the old pattern show up? What did I learn? What needs forgiveness (of myself or others)? What needs repair? What amends might I need to make? This mirrors The Holland Method teaching: We don't shame the pattern, we bring it into awareness. The evening review isn't about judgment or perfection. It's about integration, bringing the day full circle so wisdom can emerge. When you acknowledge what happened, the wins and the slips, you complete the cycle. You metabolize the experience. And tomorrow begins clean. *This is how you build a life from the inside out.*

A Note on Consistency

You don't need to do this workbook perfectly. Some days you'll complete all nine practices. Other days you might do a few. Some days you may only pause once and journal. That's part of the process. The point isn't consistency in completing every task. It's consistency in returning and forming new habits. Each time you return to the page, to meditation, and to reflection, you reinforce the habit of returning to yourself. You're choosing to operate from a more grounded center rather than reacting from old patterns. Over time, this retrains how your nervous system responds to daily life.

Eventually, this rhythm becomes less about completing tasks and more about how you orient yourself throughout the day. It helps you stay grounded, make clearer decisions, and respond rather than react. Start with today. Use the Daily Check-In sheets and following the daily prompts. Set your four pause alarms. Commit to today only. If you miss a day or only complete part of the practice, simply resume the following day. That's the work. Let's go.

Co-Create

Second Innocence

This is not a reflection about fantasy, though wonder and imagination is the energy that moves us. It's not about manifestation, though longing and vision are treated as sacred. It's not a prosperity gospel. But abundance, in its truest form, is central. The kind of abundance measured in love, presence, faith, and connection. This reflection does not ask you to escape reality. It invites you to wake up from the false one you may already be living in.

We are born into a world that offers two paths. One calls us to remember the deeper reality: the one made of innocence, love, forgiveness, and light. The other lulls us into forgetting. It keeps us asleep in fear, in separation, in cynicism. It teaches us to trust only what can be measured or controlled, pulling us into a kind of rationalism that disconnects us from the soul.

There is a phrase found in the 12 step rooms of Adult Children of Alcoholics (ACA) that says, "second innocence is better than the first." A second innocence is about choosing the first path. It is a call to remember. To remember what you came into this world knowing: before you were taught to fear, to perform, to protect. It is not a naïve denial of pain or reality. It is a brave return to the deeper law beneath all others: love. At its core, experiencing a second innocence is about awakening, not as a finish line or spiritual accomplishment, but as a way of seeing. A practice of returning. A retraining of the mind. It is a reorientation toward what is most true, most enduring, most alive. A return to the original code.

This is an invitation to Co-create. One that includes wonder and wisdom. One that makes space for both brokenness and beauty. One that does not flinch at the world, but sees through it. All the echoes of Jesus' words ring through: the kingdom of heaven is now... in my house are many mansions... not as references to distant places, but as invitations into present states of consciousness. I talk to you, not as someone with a perfect faith, but as someone whose faith has broken and been rebuilt. Unmade and remade again. Over time, I've learned that heaven and hell are not destinations. They are lenses. They are ways of seeing, and ways of forgetting. This reflection is about choosing to see, hear, and live again. To return to the place inside you that has never been lost, only buried. To awaken not to something new, but to something eternal. To reclaim an innocence that was never ignorance, but the clearest kind of knowing.

I invite you to a Second Innocence. It's good to be home. And you're invited home too. We do this by the firm belief of "perfect love casts out fear". Will you choose to love today, yourself and those around you?

Establish Your Vision

Living Out Your Purpose

Before we begin the journey through the workbook, we must first establish a vision—a clear intention for the life you feel called to co-create and fully realize. Without a vision, we drift. We live reactively rather than intentionally. We let the patterns of the past shape the patterns of the future. But with a vision, we have direction. We have something to orient toward. We have a map that guides us home to who we were always meant to be. *This is not about setting goals or creating another to-do list.* This is about listening to the deepest part of yourself—your soul—and naming what it's asking of you. *This is not about perfection or performance.* This is about becoming. About aligning your daily life with your deepest calling. About living from the inside out.

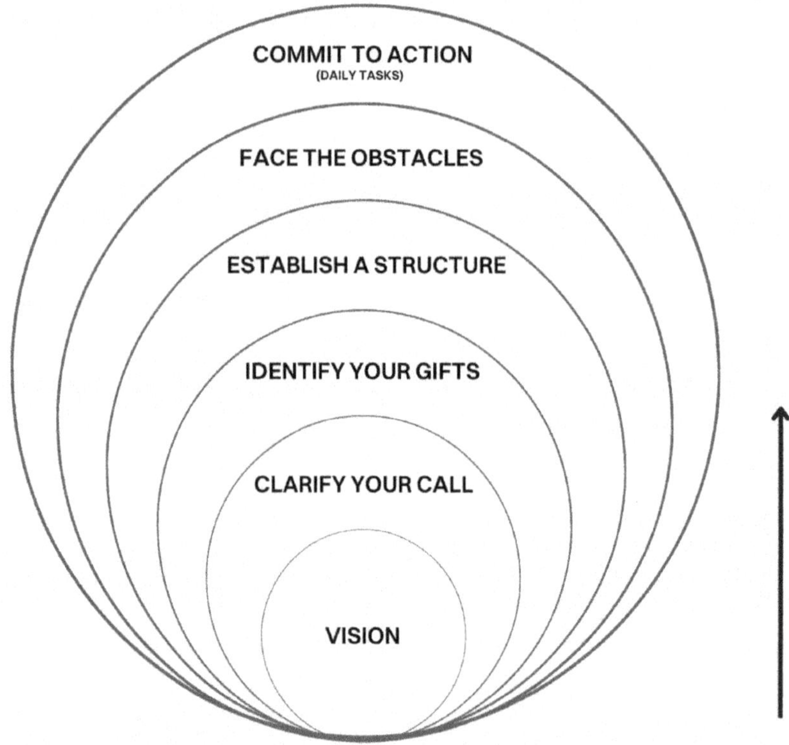

UNDERSTANDING THE VISION FRAMEWORK

The diagram on the previous page shows how your vision unfolds in concentric circles—each layer building on the one before it, moving from inner knowing to outer action.

Here's how it works:

VISION (Soul) - The core. Your deepest knowing about what you're here to do and become.

CLARIFY YOUR CALL - The first layer. Understanding what your soul is asking of you.

IDENTIFY YOUR GIFTS - The second layer. Recognizing the unique strengths you bring.

ESTABLISH A STRUCTURE - The third layer. Creating the daily framework to support your vision.

FACE THE OBSTACLES - The fourth layer. Naming what stands in the way so you can work with it.

COMMIT TO ACTION - The outermost layer. The daily tasks that bring your vision to life.

The arrow pointing upward represents growth and expansion—as you move through each layer, you're building the life you're called to live.

How to use this section:

Take your time with these questions. Don't rush. This is sacred work. As you work through each section, you'll be moving through the circles of the diagram—from the center outward. Each question helps you build the next layer.

Find a quiet space. Sit with each question. Let the answers rise naturally—not from your mind's should's and expectations, but from the a deeper knowing. You may not have all the answers right away. That's okay. Return to this section as often as you need. Your vision will clarify and evolve as you do the work.

Suggested Practice:

1. Light a candle or create a peaceful space

2. Take a few deep breaths to center yourself

3. Look at the vision diagram and notice which layer you're working on

4. Read each question slowly and dream. Allow imagination to be the practice.

5. Write what comes—without editing or censoring

6. Trust what emerges

7. As you complete each section, consider writing key words that summarize each layer. You will be asked at the end to tie it together.

STEP 1: CLARIFY YOUR CALL

The First Circle: Your Deepest Knowing

Your call is the deeper invitation of your life—the pull toward something more meaningful, more aligned, more true. It's what your soul has been whispering all along. This is the first layer radiating out from your core vision. Here, we're listening to what life is asking of you—not what others want, not what you think you should do, but what your deepest self has always wanted to do. As you answer these questions, you're building the foundation of your vision. If you're stuck or don't know, imagine. Dream big and wild.

What do I truly want?

Not what others want for you. Not what you think you should want. But what you—at the deepest level—actually desire.

____

____

____

____

____

____

____

Where am I being called?

What direction is your life asking you to move toward? What feels like the next right step, even if you can't see the whole path?

____

____

____

____

____

____

What does my deepest self ask of me?

As you listen to the voice of Love—without fear, without doubt—what is it asking you to do, to become, to offer? One helpful way to determine if it's the voice of Love is if it's gentle and kind.

____

____

____

____

____

____

____

STEP 2: IDENTIFY YOUR GIFTS

The Second Circle: Your Unique Offering

You are uniquely gifted. There are things only you can bring to the world—not because you're better than others, but because you are you. Your gifts are not just talents or skills; they're the essence of who you are when you're most alive. This layer builds on your call. Now that you know what you're being invited toward, it's time to recognize what you bring to that calling—the strengths, abilities, and qualities that are yours alone to offer.

What are my strengths?

What do you enjoy doing? What comes naturally to you? Where do you feel competent, capable, confident?

____

____

____

____

____

____

What has my particular life prepared me to give?

If I trusted that my specific journey—with all its gifts and wounds—was preparation for something, what would that be?

____

____

____

____

____

____

____

____

STEP 3: ESTABLISH A STRUCTURE

The Third Circle: Your Daily Framework

Vision without structure remains fantasy. To live your vision, you must shape your daily life to support it. This is where intention meets action. This layer is about creating the container for your vision. You know your call. You know your gifts. Now: how will you organize your life so that your vision can actually be lived—not just imagined?

How must I shape my life to support this vision?

What needs to change in how you spend your time, energy, and resources? What structures need to be put in place?

____

____

____

____

____

____

____

What specific changes need to happen for this vision to become fulfilled?

Be specific. What habits need to shift? What commitments need to be made or released? What boundaries need to be established?

____

____

____

____

____

____

____

____

What daily commitments will bring it into being?

Your vision will be realized through daily practice. What will you commit to doing each day to move toward this vision? Examples: Morning meditation, writing two pages of a book, a song/verse a day, an hour of study?

____

____

____

____

____

____

____

____

____

STEP 4: FACE THE OBSTACLES

The Fourth Circle: What Stands in the Way

Every vision encounters resistance—both external and internal. Naming the obstacles gives you power over them. What you can see, you can work with. You've clarified your call, identified your gifts, and established a structure. But something will inevitably get in the way—fear, old patterns, external constraints especially financial fear. Almost always financial.

What am I resisting?

Where do you feel internal pushback? What part of this vision scares you? What are you avoiding?

____

____

____

____

____

____

What's getting in my way?

What internal patterns sabotage you? What beliefs hold you back? Common obstacles: fear of failure, fear of success, limiting beliefs ("I'm not enough"), past wounds, lack of financial means and support, practical constraints.

____

____

____

____

____

____

____

____

STEP 5: COMMIT TO ACTION

The Outermost Circle: Living It Daily

Vision becomes reality through committed action. Not someday. Not when everything is perfect. Now. This is the outermost layer—where your vision meets the world. All the inner work you've done now translates into concrete, daily action. This is how you live out your purpose.

What action will I take this week to move toward my vision?

Be specific. What is one concrete step you can take in the next seven days?

____

____

____

____

What support do I need?

You don't have to do this alone. Who or what will help you stay committed? Accountability partner? Community? Resources?

____

____

____

I Commit To:

In your own words, declare your commitment to this vision. Be honest. Be specific. Example: "I will show up for this vision daily, trusting the process even when I can't see the outcome. I will honor my gifts, face my obstacles, and take the next right step. This vision is worthy of my devotion. I am ready to begin."

____

____

____

____

Signature: ________________________________

Date: ___________________________________

YOUR VISION SUMMARY

Bringing It All Together

Now that you've worked through all five circles—from the center outward—it's time to distill your vision into a clear, concise statement that you can return to daily. Look back at the diagram. You've moved from the core (your vision) through each expanding layer, building a complete framework for living out your purpose. This summary page helps you capture the essence of all that work in a form you can use every day.

My Vision Statement

In 2-4 sentences, capture the essence of what you're moving toward. This is your North Star. *Example: "I am creating a life of presence, purpose, and creative expression. I am using my gifts to serve others while honoring my need for rest and connection. I am becoming the grounded, authentic person I was always meant to be."*

____

____

____

Daily Affirmation Based on My Vision

Create a short affirmation (1-2 sentences) that captures your vision. You'll use this in your daily practice. *Example: "I am aligned with my calling. I trust the process of becoming."*

____

____

LIVING YOUR VISION

Your vision is now established. But a vision is not static—it's alive. It grows and evolves as you do. This represents the ongoing journey of growth—as you live your vision, you expand. You become more of who you were always meant to be. Your vision is a living practice, not a finished product. Return to these pages regularly and use the following page as your North star. Review your vision weekly (look at the diagram and check in with each layer) Revise it as needed. Notice where you're living it—and where you're not. Remember that you don't need to have it all figured out. Clarity comes through action, not before it. Trust the unfolding. Your vision is already calling you forward. The circles expand as you grow—there's always more depth to discover. Use the diagram as a touchstone. When you feel lost, return to the center: What is my core vision? When you feel stuck, check which layer needs attention: Is it structure? Obstacles? Action? When you feel aligned, notice which circles feel most alive—that's where you're growing. The work begins now.

Now on the next page review everything you have written and write out (in pencil) the following levels / stages of Your Vision.

VISION

____

____

____

CALL // PURPOSE

____

____

GIFTS // TALENTS

____

____

STRUCTURE

____

____

OBSTACLES

____

____

ACTION STEPS

____

____

One

The Work

A Daily Rhythm

This first week is about getting into a flow and groove with this material. Before we dive into the problem, the solution, and the nine states of transformation, we must first establish the practice itself, the daily rhythm that will carry you through this entire process. "The Work" is not about adding more to your already full life. **It's about creating a structure that brings you back to yourself each day**, a sacred container where transformation can actually occur. Think of it as tuning your instrument before you play. Without this daily calibration, you'll continue living from old patterns, reacting from the smaller self, and missing the quiet voice of your soul. This week, you'll establish morning and evening practices and build the habit of pausing throughout the day. You'll discover that consistency, not intensity, is what rewires the nervous system and opens the pathway to the Larger Self. Some of these practices may feel simple, even too basic. But simplicity is the point. Daily devotion creates the structure for the change you're seeking.

What does "The Work" actually mean? The Work is not about more effort or control. That only creates strain and blocks. Watch children at play, they don't "work" at it. They simply play and are free. The Work is creating space to play again. It's creating a container to come alive again. Our soul naturally wants freedom: to express, to be vibrant, to feel alive. Paradoxically, it's the ego that prevents us from actually playing. The smaller self is so busy managing, controlling, and protecting that it forgets how to be free. Work and play are not opposites. In their truest form, they're synonymous with joy. It is devotion, instead of labor. It's a singular focus to fulfill your vision.

Here's the truth: *You don't have to mine for the gold when you are the gold.*

In the beginning, there's nothing but a clean slate, an open field with seeds to plant. There's so much to be done, so much to construct. The structure isn't yet livable. But here's the secret: The play is enjoying the whole process. It's like building a fort as a kid. The building itself is the fun. The Work is devotion paired with belief that what you're creating is already accomplished. Yes, there's a process. But you bring total commitment to the truth that this vibrancy, this dream, this vision inside you is waiting to be fulfilled. **Your purpose, your calling, and your joy are directly linked. They are the same.** So as you move through this workbook, remember: you're not laboring under burden. You're building the fort. You're planting the seeds. You're playing in the field of your own becoming. And that is The Work. By the end of this week, you'll have a rhythm you can return to for the rest of this workbook—and hopefully for the rest of your life. This is where it all begins.

Mod 1 // Day 1

Reading

The central purpose of this workbook, if summarized in a few sentences, is this: **to help you see yourself clearly—who you really are**. To help you identify how you would live differently without fear. And to retrain your thought system from fear to love. To assist in these goals, we need a plan and a process, which is the purpose of these daily check-ins.

But before we proceed further, it's important to connect with your vision—one that is deeply personal and uniquely yours to live out. In many ways, this process is about waking up. In the twelve-step community, this is described as *having had a spiritual awakening as a result of these steps*. Marianne Williamson reflects on this same idea in her book *The Mystic Jesus*, noting that **humanity is often described as being asleep—and that when God put Adam to sleep before creating Eve, the Scriptures never explicitly state that he woke up.** This process is designed to help you not only wake up, but to live out that inner calling and purpose. Spend at least 10 minutes this morning with the dreamer within. But rather than simply imagining what you want or setting goals to achieve, I invite you to feel what it would be like as if your vision is already fulfilled. Not "someday I'll do this," but "this is who I am now." If fear was not present, what would you be doing? What have you wanted to do? Feel yourself living in that reality. Notice what images and visions come forth, and write them down. Pay particular attention to any negative voices and feelings that arise. Notice both the dreamer and the inner critic.

Journaling

What am I believing and experiencing today (emotionally, physically and spiritually)? What is my positive mindset and my negative mindset? How can I reparent myself with my current situation? What would the voice of Love say?

Vision

Reconnect to your Vision // What structure and implemenation needs to occur today?

____

____

Meditation

Dawnos _Oriented_ Album // Track 1 – Vision & Purpose

Affirmation

Morning Affirmation ______________________________   Evening Affirmation ________________________________

Pausing (Write out the times // set alarms)

Morning ____________   Midday ____________   Afternoon ____________   Evening ____________

Physical Movement

Walking, Yoga, Running, Weight lifting, Stretching, Jiu Jitsu, Pilates, or another: ______________

Resistance (Tasks for the Day)

Creative ____

Professional ____

Relationship(s) ____

Self ____

Evening Review

How did it go? What lesson(s) did I learn? Who do I need to make an amends with or forgive?

____

____

Mod 1 // Day 2

Reading

So how do you trust a vision, this deeper knowing and intuition within you? You begin with discernment. First: is it coming from love or fear? Is this the mind of love speaking, or the mind of fear? Second: does it create expansion or restriction? Does it lead toward a larger way of living, a widening of self, possibility, and presence? Often, true expansion carries an edge of risk. There is risk in what it will take to carry this through. Third: is there energy there, an aliveness? Do you want to do this, not from a place of "should"? Does something in you come alive when you imagine it? Fourth: is it in service to something beyond yourself? Is there purpose here, a meaning that connects your life to others and to the world? These questions help clarify your intuition with the vision. They reveal whether you can trust it. **LEAP is a framework: Love, Expansion, Aliveness, and Purpose.**

When you can honestly say yes to these, how could you be moving in the wrong direction? Where is the mistake in love, expansion, vitality, and meaning? Once you know this, you have your path. But knowing alone isn't enough. This is where many people break down, not because the vision was wrong, but because they weren't willing to live it. Every meaningful path requires practice. A resolve and willingness to stay when it gets uncomfortable. This is the path and the practice. Practice requires focus by forming new habits and then holding steady when fear, ego, or external circumstances try to pull you off course. Staying with the work when doubt whispers, *Is this worth it?* But when it comes down to it, what mistake could you possibly make when you're aligned with love, expansion, aliveness, and purpose?

For me, this workbook and meditations are a testament to that process. I could not have seen them through without it. What you're holding came from two years of daily devotion: writing, thinking, creating, and recording. There were many early mornings and late evenings. There were many setbacks and moments of questioning whether it was worth pursuing. But I knew I had to do it. Everything here was born from that knowing and the willingness to practice it.

Journaling

What am I believing and experiencing today (emotionally, physically and spiritually)? What is my positive mindset and my negative mindset? How can I reparent myself with my current situation? What would the voice of Love say?

Vision

Reconnect to your Vision // What structure and implemenation needs to occur today?

____

____

Meditation

Dawnos *Oriented* Album // Track 2 – Ocean Breath

Affirmation

Morning Affirmation ______________________________   Evening Affirmation ______________________________

Pausing (Write out the times // set alarms)

Morning _____________   Midday _____________   Afternoon _____________   Evening _____________

Physical Movement

Walking, Yoga, Running, Weight lifting, Stretching, Jiu Jitsu, Pilates, or another: _______________

Resistance (Tasks for the Day)

Creative ____

Professional ____

Relationship(s) ____

Self ____

Evening Review

How did it go? What lesson(s) did I learn? Who do I need to make an amends with or forgive?

____

____

Mod 1 // Day 3

Reading

What if the most powerful tool for calming your mind and regulating your nervous system was something you already have, something you're doing right now without even thinking about it? Let's talk about breathwork—the foundation, the bedrock of meditation. When we're stationary, we're only using 10% of our lung capacity. By bringing more attention to the breath, we're able to expand our oxygen intake, which engages oxygen levels throughout the body. On the physiological side, when you breathe more deeply, you bring more vitality to the body because the breath is like fuel for energy. More oxygen means better circulation and energy production in your cells. It can also lower your heart rate and blood pressure, and reduce cortisol levels. For example, if you practice the fire breath exercise or meditation from the Dawnos meditations, you'll feel a tingling and buzz in your body after the breath exercise. It's like a massive surge of energy and vitality. On the emotional side, conscious and mindful breathwork helps reduce anxiety and allows you to feel more calm. It activates the parasympathetic nervous system, which takes you out of the sympathetic nervous system—fight, flight, freeze, fawn mode—into a rest and digest mode. This allows you to not only digest food, but digest the energy you're holding.

A simple visual practice is to picture the ocean tide and allow your body to get in sync with the waves—the breath going in and out, like the tide. This allows you to enter a state of flow. Because the whole point is this: **When you're in sync with your breath, when your mind is fully attuned and noticing your breath, this state of flow allows you to be present to what is.** It gets you out of the trance and back to the present moment. The link to the breath is the first step of flow. When you're anxious, your breath is shallow and rapid. When you're stressed, you might even hold your breath without realizing it. But when you consciously deepen and slow your breath, your body relaxes. Your mind clears. You return to yourself. This is how you get into flow.

Journaling

What am I believing and experiencing today (emotionally, physically and spiritually)? What is my positive mindset and my negative mindset? How can I reparent myself with my current situation? What would the voice of Love say?

____

____

____

____

____

____

Vision

Reconnect to your Vision // What structure and implemenation needs to occur today?

____

____

Meditation

Dawnos _Oriented_ Album // Track 3 – Inner Temple

Affirmation

Morning Affirmation ______________________________   Evening Affirmation _______________________________

Pausing (Write out the times // set alarms)

Morning ______________   Midday ______________   Afternoon ______________   Evening ______________

Physical Movement

Walking, Yoga, Running, Weight lifting, Stretching, Jiu Jitsu, Pilates, or another: ______________

Resistance (Tasks for the Day)

Creative ____

Professional ____

Relationship(s) ____

Self ____

Evening Review

How did it go? What lesson(s) did I learn? Who do I need to make an amends with or forgive?

____

____

Mod 1 // Day 4

Reading

Maybe there are days when you wonder if everything you're doing will ever come together. Maybe you've been looking for a new job and haven't found it after a year of applying. Maybe you're working to become a musician and singer-songwriter, and no record label or record deal has materialized. Or maybe you're longing so deeply for a companion, to be married and have children, and none of that has happened yet. It could be one of those days when you're just wondering: What am I doing? Will this ever shift? Will it ever shift for me?

It's on these days when we need to especially stay focused on the deepest core of our vision. The question becomes: What is my deepest self, my soul, asking of me? Have I found that connection? If I go inward, I can at least connect to purpose—an anchor amid all the unanswered questions. You may ask, "But I don't even know what my deepest self is asking." Then here is where the practice comes in. The Work of sitting, asking, praying, and especially listening becomes so important. Become deeply focused on that one question: What is my deepest self asking of me? You may simply pray: God, show me. Make clear my best and highest purpose. Please guide me. I have heard this prayer in Al-Anon that says, **"Reveal to me what needs to be revealed, and heal in me what needs to be healed."** And then be still and stay open. Notice what you would tell a friend in this same situation. These words are often from your voice of Love. Write those words out for yourself. It is so easy to question and get stuck in the worries of the future or the regrets of the past—worries that hold you from the present moment. We cannot perceive our path without an internal Light illuminating for us our deepest calling and purpose. All we have to do is ask, listen, and trust.

Journaling

What am I believing and experiencing today (emotionally, physically and spiritually)? What is my positive mindset and my negative mindset? How can I reparent myself with my current situation? What would the voice of Love say?

____

____

____

____

____

____

____

____

Vision

Reconnect to your Vision // What structure and implemenation needs to occur today?

____

____

Meditation

Dawnos _Oriented_ Album // Track 1 – Vision & Purpose

Affirmation

Morning Affirmation _______________________________   Evening Affirmation _______________________________

Pausing (Write out the times // set alarms)

Morning _____________   Midday _____________   Afternoon _____________   Evening _____________

Physical Movement

Walking, Yoga, Running, Weight lifting, Stretching, Jiu Jitsu, Pilates, or another: _______________

Resistance (Tasks for the Day)

Creative ____

Professional ____

Relationship(s) ____

Self ____

Evening Review

How did it go? What lesson(s) did I learn? Who do I need to make an amends with or forgive?

____

____

Mod 1 // Day 5

Reading

When it comes to obstacles—and you can be sure they will come—see them as gifts. See them as your specialized curriculum. Not to block you, but to purify and sharpen the edge of you mastering your talents to fulfill the vision. Do not be troubled by the obstacles. **Every hero in every great story must face the trials.** This is the way. So the practice is to see them as friends. See through them to what they're really offering you. Here's the practice: when you encounter an obstacle, go back to your calling. Trust that your calling is for a higher purpose. You know it's of the higher purpose when it's not just for yourself, but for the expansion of those around you in love. This gives meaning to everything—even the obstacles. And in the moment of the immediate obstacle, really sit with it. Get creative with it. See it as an opportunity. It's all a frame of mind.

Every great person is challenged. But the challenge is helping you master the resistance. That's what you're here to work with. The obstacle is not the enemy. **The obstacle is the teacher.** It's showing you where you still need to grow, where you still need to sharpen your skills, where you still need to deepen your trust. When you reframe obstacles this way, they lose their power to stop you. They become part of the journey, not barriers to it. They become the very thing that makes you capable of fulfilling your vision. So today, if you're facing an obstacle, pause. Ask yourself: What is this here to teach me? How is this sharpening me? How is this preparing me for what's ahead? Then get creative. Sit with it. Work with it. See it as a friend who's come to make you stronger, wiser, more masterful. The resistance is not there to defeat you. It's there to refine you. And when you master the resistance, you become unstoppable. This is how heroes are made. This is how visions are fulfilled. This is how you become who you're meant to be.

Journaling

What am I believing and experiencing today (emotionally, physically and spiritually)? What is my positive mindset and my negative mindset? How can I reparent myself with my current situation? What would the voice of Love say?

____

____

____

____

____

____

____

Vision

Reconnect to your Vision // What structure and implemenation needs to occur today?

____

____

Meditation

Dawnos *Oriented* Album // Track 2 – Ocean Breath

Affirmation

Morning Affirmation _______________________________   Evening Affirmation _______________________________

Pausing (Write out the times // set alarms)

Morning _____________   Midday _____________   Afternoon _____________   Evening _____________

Physical Movement

Walking, Yoga, Running, Weight lifting, Stretching, Jiu Jitsu, Pilates, or another: _______________

Resistance (Tasks for the Day)

Creative ____

Professional ____

Relationship(s) ____

Self ____

Evening Review

How did it go? What lesson(s) did I learn? Who do I need to make an amends with or forgive?

____

____

Mod 1 // Day 6

Reading

Living out one's vision and seeing it through requires a fierce determination to see and listen in a new way. In essence, to fulfill your vision requires you to go on a hero's journey—both inward and outward—that will lead you to face your own dragons. These metaphorical dragons are the images, thoughts, and emotional states the ego casts in front of you to keep you small. It is the ego that is afraid of love and abundance, because the ego mind cannot understand oneness with God, others, and oneself. To the ego mind—one's own mind of fear—it feels reckless, impossible, and irrational (even silly) to follow the path of love.

The good news is that once you set a foot on the path, hidden hands will appear to assist you on your journey. These hidden hands come in the form of encouragement, opening of doors, and opportunities you couldn't have possibly imagined. It is important to note that you are not alone on this journey, and that you will be given everything you need to complete and fulfill this vision. Now, the fear of failure is the ego's continual battle cry to keep you small. **The voice of Love is always gentle and kind,** inviting you to largeness and expansion. As C.S. Lewis asked, why would we choose to stay in a sandbox in the backyard when we can go out on the beach of unlimited sand? Such is the opportunity when we stay connected to the mind of love. Remember this: depression occurs when we allow the cloud of fear to obscure our vision. It takes great devotion to maintain one's focus on the daily task to see this vision into reality. It's here for the taking.

Journaling

What am I believing and experiencing today (emotionally, physically and spiritually)? What is my positive mindset and my negative mindset? How can I reparent myself with my current situation? What would the voice of Love say?

____

____

____

____

____

____

____

____

Vision

Reconnect to your Vision // What structure and implemenation needs to occur today?

____

____

Meditation

Dawnos _Oriented_ Album // Track 3 – Inner Temple

Affirmation

Morning Affirmation ______________________________   Evening Affirmation _______________________________

Pausing   (Write out the times // set alarms)

Morning ______________   Midday ______________   Afternoon ______________   Evening ______________

Physical Movement

Walking, Yoga, Running, Weight lifting, Stretching, Jiu Jitsu, Pilates, or another: ________________

Resistance (Tasks for the Day)

Creative ____

Professional ____

Relationship(s) ____

Self ____

Evening Review

How did it go? What lesson(s) did I learn? Who do I need to make an amends with or forgive?

____

____

Reading

We cannot enjoy peace if we serve two masters. The two masters are the mind of fear and the mind of Love. The mind of fear is constant. It sends a continuous signal of messages and images, luring each of us to believe it offers the solution—through a romantic relationship, a successful career, a beautiful home, adventurous trips with the family, and so on. None of those elements are bad in and of themselves. They just aren't the solution and answer. The answer lies in living unattached to those elements as *the* thing. All day long, throughout the day, the ego—the mind of fear—will send these images and messages. That's why affirmations are vital, of utmost importance. **Affirmations are like a tether holding you to truth and love.** The ego projects both incredible, tempting images of pseudo-fulfillment, and then, on the flip of a switch, nightmare scenarios of fear. It's relentless and constant.

Fortunately, we always have a way out. I love this quote by Pema Chödrön: "We are one blink of an eye away from being fully awake." Awakening means to listen and to see from the mind of Love. The mind of Love is always available, yet often clouded by the mind of fear. A practice today is to journal the most loving message the voice of Love would say. Such as: *I am safe. I'm okay today. I am loved. I am enough.* This is your tether and anchor to Source. When the mind of fear sends its images—the seductive promises or the terrifying threats—you have something to hold onto. Not by fighting the fear, but by returning to love. The affirmations aren't about positive thinking or wishful thinking. They're about remembering what's true. They're about cutting through the noise fear sends out and tuning back into the frequency of love.

Journaling

What am I believing and experiencing today (emotionally, physically and spiritually)? What is my positive mindset and my negative mindset? How can I reparent myself with my current situation? What would the voice of Love say?

____

____

____

____

____

____

____

____

Vision

Reconnect to your Vision // What structure and implemenation needs to occur today?

____

____

Meditation

Dawnos *Air* Album // Track 1 – Box Breath

Affirmation

Morning Affirmation ________________________   Evening Affirmation ____________________________

Pausing   (Write out the times // set alarms)

Morning ____________   Midday ____________   Afternoon ____________   Evening ____________

Physical Movement

Walking, Yoga, Running, Weight lifting, Stretching, Jiu Jitsu, Pilates, or another: ______________

Resistance (Tasks for the Day)

Creative ____

Professional ____

Relationship(s) ____

Self ____

Evening Review

How did it go? What lesson(s) did I learn? Who do I need to make an amends with or forgive?

____

____

Notes:

Two

The Problem

A Virtual Reality

Most of us move through life living in what we might call a "little r" reality—a virtual reality built from years of conditioning, past experiences, and learned interpretations. From this limited perspective, we no longer see life as it actually is. We see it through a distorted lens of fear, lack, and separation. This is the core problem: We've lost contact with Reality—capital R. But here's what makes this so insidious: our denial doesn't look like denial. It disguises itself as realism. We say, "I'm just being realistic," while carrying a mind full of fear. We believe we're seeing clearly, but we're actually seeing through the lens of the smaller self—one that whispers: *"I'm not enough. This can't change. I have to do this alone."* These mantras feel like truth. But they're just thoughts. And when we don't question them, we fall into spiritual amnesia—we forget who we are and what's already within us. We're not denying pain. We're denying possibility. We're not denying hardship. We're denying wholeness. We're denying the deeper Reality beneath the noise.

Here's what this looks like in daily life: You're sitting across from someone you love. Sunlight streams through the window, casting warmth across their face. They're sharing something meaningful, something beautiful. But you're not really there. You're replaying yesterday's conversation, worrying about tomorrow's meeting, lost in a story about what they think of you. You're not present. You're not here. And because you're not here, you miss it. You miss the gift of this moment. You miss the love that's actually available. You miss your own life. This is one of the most dangerous forms of denial: the denial of the present moment. We convince ourselves that peace comes later—once everything is resolved, once we've achieved enough, once we've become enough. But the truth is simpler and more profound: you don't have to wait. You can be okay here, now—even in the middle of the mess.

Einstein said the most important question we must ask ourselves is: *"Is the universe friendly?"* And from the fearful state, we answer: "No. I am alone. I must control. I am not enough." But what if that's the lie? What if the wholeness you're seeking has never left? What if the love you're chasing is already here? What if the peace you long for is your natural state? **The problem is not that you're broken. The problem is that you can't see yourself clearly.** You've been living in a virtual reality, a fear-based simulation, for so long that you've forgotten what's real. Throughout this module, we'll explore the problem—not to shame you, but to help you see what's actually running beneath the surface. The thoughts that feel like truth but are actually fear. The beliefs that feel like realism but are actually denial. This week, we begin to wake up from that trance. We learn to recognize when we're living in the little r reality of fear and separation—and how to return to the capital R Reality of presence, love, and wholeness. The problem is clear. Now let's move toward the solution.

Mod 2 // Day 1

Reading

While we face real challenges, **we do not have to abandon ourselves**—not consciously, nor willingly. Yet we abandon ourselves every time we obsess over fears, rehearse imagined futures, project onto others, or absorb the emotions and projections they place on us. Self-abandonment looks like this subtle drifting: away from presence, away from truth, away from the body, and into a mind that loops, rehearses, and tries to control. This ego-mind, this "old thought system," as *A Course in Miracles* names it, runs on fear. It builds a nightmare out of past data points, memories, and unresolved stories. It weaves a movie reel that plays in the background of consciousness, convincing and familiar—not because it is true, but because it is practiced. The nightmare looks real because the mind is using old footage. But naming this is essential. Because until the problem is clearly understood, we remain in the denial of self that Tara Brach points to as a "trance of separation." It is simply how we have learned to imagine. The solution is not complicated, but it is not casual either. It requires diligence. It requires fierce determination. It requires a plan. The commitment is this: **I will not abandon myself here.** You choose not to entertain the thoughts that pull you into fear. You choose not to live inside the nightmare or mistake projection for reality. Instead, you return. You come back to the present moment. You come back to the body. You come back to breath.

You come back to Source. "Be still and know that I am Yahweh." Even the sacred name Yahweh becomes a prayer of returning—inhaling Yah, exhaling Weh—a reminder that presence itself is communion. And when the nightmare feels strong—when the ego insists on running its reel—you ask for help: Spirit, free me from my own mind. Free me from the old thought system. For thoughts of fear are the opposite of the vision God—or Source, however you name it—has given me. Fear's imagination is a counterfeit. God's imagination is the real thing: quiet, generative, spacious, unifying. Sometimes the shift comes through a single symbol—a light, a face, an image of Jesus—a reminder that you can choose another movie. You can watch a new reel. You can return to a vision not born of fear. This is the work of taking "every thought captive," as the Scriptures state—not through repression, but through recognition. Through remembering. Because reality is not the nightmare. Reality is what remains when the nightmare dissolves.

Journaling

What am I believing and experiencing today (emotionally, physically and spiritually)? What is my positive mindset and my negative mindset? How can I reparent myself with my current situation? What would the voice of Love say?

Vision

Reconnect to your Vision // What structure and implemenation needs to occur today?

____

____

Meditation

Dawnos *Air* Album // Track 2 – Downshift

Affirmation

Morning Affirmation ______________________________   Evening Affirmation ______________________________

Pausing (Write out the times // set alarms)

Morning _____________   Midday _____________   Afternoon _____________   Evening _____________

Physical Movement

Walking, Yoga, Running, Weight lifting, Stretching, Jiu Jitsu, Pilates, or another: _______________

Resistance (Tasks for the Day)

Creative ____

Professional ____

Relationship(s) ____

Self ____

Evening Review

How did it go? What lesson(s) did I learn? Who do I need to make an amends with or forgive?

____

____

Mod 2 // Day 2

Reading

The mind of fear creates such a convincing state of hallucination that appears real and certain. The mind of Love is quieter, yet always available—provided that I am open and willing to see this situation differently. There have been so many occasions where I look back at times in my life, and if I could talk to my younger self, I would tell him, "You really don't have to worry at all. It will all work out." The mind of fear robs us of the joys of the day. So what is the solution?

The solution is much more of a process than a formula, but it is comprised of getting still, going inward, and paradoxically inviting in the negative belief with a willingness to see and hear one's situation through the mind of Love. This isn't easy, and often I experience heightened emotions at first. But when I am with it long enough, breathing through it, asking myself if this is actually true right now and asking the Spirit for help and guidance—something shifts. There is something that happens when I surrender my expectation of what is to happen: a softer awareness of love around me. Often there is that ever-still small voice saying, "I've got you. Everything will be okay."

Last night, I had a situation where I slowly built up very upsetting scenarios in my mind. In fact, I was running through so many worst-case scenarios, convinced this fear would happen. I would try to challenge it, but the fear was so strong. When the situation passed—none of the fearful projections occurred. In fact, it was the opposite. This morning, as I reflect, I realize several things. One, it's understandable that this happened because I was hurt in this area of my life years ago in the ways I was "hallucinating" with these negative stories I was telling myself. Two, sometimes these moments and situations have to run their course. And three, here is an opportunity for gentle inquiry—to see this as a hurt and wounded younger self that needs love.

Journaling

What am I believing and experiencing today (emotionally, physically and spiritually)? What is my positive mindset and my negative mindset? How can I reparent myself with my current situation? What would the voice of Love say?

____

____

____

____

____

____

____

Vision

Reconnect to your Vision // What structure and implemenation needs to occur today?

____

____

Meditation

Dawnos *Oriented* Album // Track 5 – Ocean Breath

Affirmation

Morning Affirmation _______________________   Evening Affirmation _________________________________

Pausing   (Write out the times // set alarms)

Morning _____________   Midday _____________   Afternoon _____________   Evening _____________

Physical Movement

Walking, Yoga, Running, Weight lifting, Stretching, Jiu Jitsu, Pilates, or another: _______________

Resistance (Tasks for the Day)

Creative ____

Professional ____

Relationship(s) ____

Self ____

Evening Review

How did it go? What lesson(s) did I learn? Who do I need to make an amends with or forgive?

____

____

Mod 2 // Day 3

Reading

When restlessness grips you—whether at 3 AM with worry spinning through your mind, or during the day when anxiety about the future pulls you into endless rumination about a difficult situation or troubled relationship—there is a simple practice that can bring immediate relief. The practice is this: become the witness by being aware of the space around you. This isn't abstract or complicated. You don't need to fight your thoughts or force yourself to calm down. Instead, you simply shift your attention from the thoughts themselves to the space around you.

Right now, as you read this, notice the room you're in. Notice the space between you and the walls. Notice the air. Notice the openness that holds everything—the furniture, the sounds, the light. This is spatial awareness, and it's always available to you. What happens when you do this? You naturally become present. The anxious thoughts don't necessarily disappear, but you're no longer trapped inside them. You've stepped back into your larger self—the part of you that can observe without being consumed, that can witness without being swept away. This is what it means to wake up from the spell of the ego. **The ego lives in the stories, the worries, the endless what-ifs. But your true self—your awareness—is like the sky that holds all weather.** Clouds come and go, but the sky remains unchanged. The beautiful thing about this practice is that it becomes a dance. You'll move in and out of these two states—sometimes identified with your thoughts, sometimes resting in spacious awareness. Both are part of being human. But knowing you can access this *witnessing* state at any moment changes everything. Think of it as bringing light into darkness. Your loving awareness is that light. And when you extend it into the space around you, you discover an unlimited supply of love, peace, and forgiveness that was there all along, waiting to be noticed. **This spatial awareness becomes like a sixth sense—a superpower that allows you to see and hear in new ways.** It breaks the trance of worry. It restores your connection to what's real and present. So today, practice this: When you feel pulled into rumination or anxiety, pause. Notice the space around you. Feel the air on your skin. Observe the room with gentle attention. Let yourself expand into that awareness. You are not your thoughts. You are the loving space in which thoughts appear. This is always true. This is always available. This is your way home.

Journaling

What am I believing and experiencing today (emotionally, physically and spiritually)? What is my positive mindset and my negative mindset? How can I reparent myself with my current situation? What would the voice of Love say?

____

____

____

____

Vision

Reconnect to your Vision // What structure and implemenation needs to occur today?

____

____

Meditation

Dawnos *Oriented* Album // Track 6 – Sacred Space

Affirmation

Morning Affirmation ___________________________   Evening Affirmation ___________________________________

Pausing   (Write out the times // set alarms)

Morning _____________   Midday _____________   Afternoon _____________   Evening _____________

Physical Movement

Walking, Yoga, Running, Weight lifting, Stretching, Jiu Jitsu, Pilates, or another: _______________

Resistance (Tasks for the Day)

Creative ____

Professional ____

Relationship(s) ____

Self ____

Evening Review

How did it go? What lesson(s) did I learn? Who do I need to make an amends with or forgive?

____

____

Mod 2 // Day 4

Reading

Regulation begins with orientation, and one of the most effective ways to orient is through creating a sense of sacred space. This practice has helped countless people settle into their bodies, emotions, and thinking, offering a way to reset and ground before entering challenging moments. Recently, a New York Times article highlighted an NBA player who credited meditation and visualization practices with helping him tune out external noise and distraction. What stood out was that during the same season he adopted these practices, his performance markedly improved—something he directly attributed to this inner work. While this isn't new information in sports psychology, it reinforces the effectiveness of intentional, embodied mental practices.

When creating a sacred space, it isn't enough to simply visualize a place that feels safe or meaningful. The practice deepens when you engage all of your senses—sight, sound, touch, smell, and the felt quality of the space itself. When this happens, the experience moves out of abstraction and into the body. The nervous system responds. Emotions soften. Thoughts begin to settle, not through effort, but through attunement.

There is a further nuance that takes this practice even deeper. As you draw the sacred space into the present moment, the two begin to merge: sacred space becomes now. The peace once associated with a particular place becomes available here. In this way, space itself functions as a kind of sixth sense—beyond sight, sound, smell, taste, and touch. **Spatial awareness creates a felt sense of connection and presence almost automatically.** How could you not be here? In a quiet and beautiful way, the same sacred space that once held you then is holding you now.

Journaling

What am I believing and experiencing today (emotionally, physically and spiritually)? What is my positive mindset and my negative mindset? How can I reparent myself with my current situation? What would the voice of Love say?

Vision

Reconnect to your Vision // What structure and implemenation needs to occur today?

____

____

Meditation

Dawnos *Air* Album // Track 5 – Space

Affirmation

Morning Affirmation _______________________   Evening Affirmation _______________________

Pausing   (Write out the times // set alarms)

Morning _____________   Midday _____________   Afternoon _____________   Evening _____________

Physical Movement

Walking, Yoga, Running, Weight lifting, Stretching, Jiu Jitsu, Pilates, or another: _______________

Resistance (Tasks for the Day)

Creative ____

Professional ____

Relationship(s) ____

Self ____

Evening Review

How did it go? What lesson(s) did I learn? Who do I need to make an amends with or forgive?

____

____

Mod 2 // Day 5

Reading

If the core problem is a sense of separation, what does that look like for each of us? The Big Book in AA talks about how the root of addiction is fear, and behind the emotion of fear is this feeling of separation and abandonment, which is formed by the ego. So, in essence, when we are caught in this trance of separation, we lose faith that we are not only being guided by a Higher Power, but fiercely loved. Think about this for a moment. Really pause and ask yourself: **Do you feel loved and in the care of God?** Do you feel connected to a higher intelligence—a higher consciousness, Source—that is working for you, not against you? If you don't, you're not alone. I think most of us, if we are honest, at some point in our lives feel as if the universe is too harsh, or that we don't deserve love—especially if we have recently made mistakes. I see this over and over with clients: this feeling of not being loved, this belief that it's hard to comprehend that we are loved when so many trials and struggles have occurred.

And of course, life is incredibly hard. Horrible events and situations do occur, and they can be gut-wrenching. And yet, the sun still rises, and good is still present in the world. It's our job—and no one else's—to rise *with* the pain and find meaning and purpose. This is character. This is the noble endeavor. Not that you or I will not make mistakes—we will. But that we still hold to this unflinching belief that we are loved, and that we will be okay. This basic okayness.

When you lose connection to this truth—when you feel abandoned, unloved, separate from Source—you are living from the ego's story. And the ego's story is always one of isolation, unworthiness, and fear. But the truth is this: **You are connected. You are being guided. You are love.** Not because you've earned it or because you've done everything right, but because that is simply what is true. It has always been true. It will always be true Your job is not to create this love or prove yourself worthy of it. Your job is to remember it, to return to it, to let it be the foundation from which you live. This is the antidote to separation. This is how you return home.

Journaling

What am I believing and experiencing today (emotionally, physically and spiritually)? What is my positive mindset and my negative mindset? How can I reparent myself with my current situation? What would the voice of Love say?

____

____

____

____

____

____

Vision

Reconnect to your Vision // What structure and implemenation needs to occur today?

____

____

Meditation

Dawnos *Air* Album // Track 4 – Expansion

Affirmation

Morning Affirmation ______________________________   Evening Affirmation ______________________________

Pausing   (Write out the times // set alarms)

Morning ______________   Midday ______________   Afternoon ______________   Evening ______________

Physical Movement

Walking, Yoga, Running, Weight lifting, Stretching, Jiu Jitsu, Pilates, or another: ______________

Resistance (Tasks for the Day)

Creative ____

Professional ____

Relationship(s) ____

Self ____

Evening Review

How did it go? What lesson(s) did I learn? Who do I need to make an amends with or forgive?

____

____

Reading

The practice of noticing and observing—of becoming the witness—is a foundational pillar within meditation. At its core, this practice invites a shift away from judgment: of situations, of others, and of ourselves. **When we judge, we subtly create separation, positioning ourselves against what is happening rather than staying present with it.** The work of witnessing is not about disengagement or avoidance, but about learning how to remain connected without being pulled into reactivity.

In traditions like Al-Anon, this way of relating is often expressed through simple phrases: "Detach with love," or "Stay on your side of the street." These sayings point to a deeper wisdom—that we are not responsible for managing other people's lives or controlling outcomes. Practically speaking, the Clouds Meditation supports this shift by helping us step out of the role of judge and into the role of observer. Rather than turning a blind eye, it offers a different vantage point: like being the blue sky instead of being caught inside the clouds, learning to see from a wider, steadier perspective rather than from within the storm.

Years ago, when my boys were young, my father and I took them to a popular pancake restaurant in Nashville. On the drive home, the boys—full of sugar—were bouncing around and arguing in the back seat, and I could feel my frustration rising. I looked over at my dad, who was completely at ease, and asked whether this didn't bother him. He smiled and said, "Boys will be boys. You and your brothers did the same thing." In that moment, **I realized his calm didn't come from the situation being different—it came from his perspective.** He wasn't in the clouds of irritation or control; he was the sky, allowing the moment to pass without being overtaken by it.

Journaling

What am I believing and experiencing today (emotionally, physically and spiritually)? What is my positive mindset and my negative mindset? How can I reparent myself with my current situation? What would the voice of Love say?

____

____

____

____

____

____

____

Vision

Reconnect to your Vision // What structure and implemenation needs to occur today?

____

____

Meditation

Dawnos _Oriented_ Album // Track 5 – Clouds

Affirmation

Morning Affirmation ______________________________   Evening Affirmation ______________________________

Pausing   (Write out the times // set alarms)

Morning ______________   Midday ______________   Afternoon ______________   Evening ______________

Physical Movement

Walking, Yoga, Running, Weight lifting, Stretching, Jiu Jitsu, Pilates, or another: ______________

Resistance (Tasks for the Day)

Creative ____

Professional ____

Relationship(s) ____

Self ____

Evening Review

How did it go? What lesson(s) did I learn? Who do I need to make an amends with or forgive?

____

____

Mod 2 // Day 7

Reading

Take some time this morning and allow yourself to recall some stressful situations—particularly times when you felt completely lost and in darkness. Times when you were convinced that what was happening would finally break you. Maybe it was fear of financial ruin, illness, or the deep-down belief that you wouldn't make it beyond whatever situation occurred in your mind. Now see and let yourself feel and realize: you are here. And in one piece. Sure, you may have some wounds, but those too can only be found in mental memories. Beyond the past, you are here. And this "here" is actually wholeness. What I mean and intend to say is this: while we are certainly tested, and the tests can be intense with extreme heat, mastery happens when you can see past it and hold to the light—both in you and outside you. It's like you are channeling a stronger existence of being as you experience and go through another passage of time that feels like a nightmare, especially when you are in it, but you are in fact fine the whole time. The mind of fear interprets life a certain way and it feels 100% real. Picture for a moment a peaceful nature scene. Maybe it's a stream in the mountains or the ocean. Close your eyes and notice what scene shows up. Take in all the sights and sounds. Do that for a moment before you read the next lines.

Now picture the same scene. But this time, allow yourself to hear and create scary music in the background—deep notes from an organ or ominous and foreboding sounds. Notice that immediately, the very place of peace changed. All in the way you create and interpret it. And the whole time, the "you" behind it remained unchanging. Both the peaceful state and the foreboding state are creations of you and your mind. So which mind do you choose to live from today? The mind of fear or the mind of Love? The mind of Love is what is actually here right now. When you realize this—that you are the one creating the soundtrack, the interpretation, the meaning—everything changes. You see that most of your suffering comes not from what's happening, but from how your mind is interpreting what's happening. The circumstances are the circumstances. But the fear? The dread? The certainty of doom? That's the mind of fear doing its work. And you can choose differently. You've survived every dark moment you thought would destroy you. You've made it through every trial you were certain you couldn't endure. You're still here and capable of choosing love over fear. So today, when fear tries to add ominous music to your life, pause. Notice what's actually happening versus what your fearful mind is creating. Choose the mind of Love. This is mastery.

Journaling

What am I believing and experiencing today (emotionally, physically and spiritually)? What is my positive mindset and my negative mindset? How can I reparent myself with my current situation? What would the voice of Love say?

____

____

____

____

Vision

Reconnect to your Vision // What structure and implemenation needs to occur today?

____

____

Meditation

Dawnos _Oriented_ Album // Track 4 – Virtual Reality

Affirmation

Morning Affirmation ___________________________   Evening Affirmation ___________________________________

Pausing   (Write out the times // set alarms)

Morning _____________   Midday _____________   Afternoon _____________   Evening _____________

Physical Movement

Walking Yoga, Running, Weightlighting, Stretching: ________________

Resistance (Tasks for the Day)

Creative ____

Professional ____

Relationship ____

Self ____

Evening Review

How did it go? What lesson(s) did I learn? Who do I need to make an amends with or forgive?

____

____

Notes:

Three

The Solution

A Move Inward

Here's the remarkable truth: the solution is simpler than you think. It's not about massive healing journeys, years of therapy, or perfecting yourself before you can finally be whole. It's not about fixing what's broken or curing what's sick. The solution is remembering—remembering who you already are, what's already within you, your original innocence. Remembering that you've never actually been separate from the wholeness you've been seeking.

An old mentor once told me something I've never forgotten. I asked him, *"What's the secret of the 12 steps? What makes this path so mystical, so profoundly healing for so many people?"* He said simply, *"It's learning to sit with yourself."* That's it. Not complicated techniques. Not years of processing. Just learning to sit with yourself. And yes—when we sit with ourselves, we're faced with the images of the mind: the shadows of fear, the old stories, the painful memories.

But here's what we also discover—the solution is right there with us. We have love. We have light. We already have what we need. The solution is accessing Source. Not forcing anything. Not manufacturing insight or engineering transformation. Not pushing or striving our way into wholeness. Because there's nothing to force—you're already whole. As James Hollis says, *"You are not a disease to be cured."* You are not a pathology to be treated.

The real issue was never addiction, depression, or anxiety. It was never your behaviors or your patterns. Disconnection is the problem—and connection is the solution. Disconnection from Source. From yourself. From the present moment. From the truth of who you are. And the path back isn't complicated. It's presence. It's breath. It's stillness. It's the willingness to turn inward instead of constantly reaching outward. The solution is a move inward—not because you're broken and need fixing, but because you're whole and need to remember. Not because something is missing, but because you've forgotten what's already here.

Throughout this module, we'll explore what it means to connect to Source—to the deeper reality beneath the noise of the conditioned mind. We'll practice dropping beneath the virtual reality of fear, shame, and separation. By returning to the deeper Reality of presence, love, and wholeness. Accessing Source isn't about achieving some elevated spiritual state. It's about softening. The mansion you've been searching for? You're already inside it. You've been inside it all along—as James Finley has beautifully described. This week, we learn to see with new eyes. To listen with new ears. To return to the place we never actually left. The solution isn't far off. It's right here. Let's begin.

Mod 3 // Day 1

Reading

Begin by thinking of someone you love deeply—someone who brings immense joy to your life, or who has brought such joy. Feel the warmth of that love, its depth and tenderness. Now imagine loving yourself with that same intensity, that same unconditional acceptance. This is not selfish—it is essential. **When you direct love and compassion toward yourself, you ignite a fire within.** You are pouring fuel on the flame of your own being. Remember this truth: You are light unto the world, and so am I. All of us are, if we are willing to receive the light then naturally we can reflect the light to others. And from that place, we will naturally turn away from what diminishes us. Darkness.

So what does this mean and how to we practically live this out? Light, which is love, is your purpose. That's it. Therefore, this is a time to awaken—to live in the light. At this moment, this hour, allow yourself to close your eyes and focus on this one belief, this one affirmation: *I am light. God (the mind of Love) is the light within me.* Notice what happens in your thoughts, emotions, and physical body as you hold this truth. Naturally, the ego (the mind of fear) will still cast its darkness before you. This is normal. Your practice is to stay focused on the light. It is from this source that your true thoughts, emotions, and physical responses emerge. This light is the energy that moves us. Our only task is to be open to it, to sit in it, and to remain open to it. Carry this with you today: You are not seeking the light. You are the light, remembering itself. If it helps, remember that childhood song, *"This little light of mine, I am going to let it shine!"*

Journaling

What am I believing and experiencing today (emotionally, physically and spiritually)? What is my positive mindset and my negative mindset? How can I reparent myself with my current situation? What would the voice of Love say?

____

____

____

____

____

____

____

____

____

Vision

Reconnect to your Vision // What structure and implemenation needs to occur today?

____

____

Meditation

Dawnos *Oriented* Album // Track 9 - Healing Light

Affirmation

Morning Affirmation ____________________________   Evening Affirmation ____________________________

Pausing   (Write out the times // set alarms)

Morning ____________   Midday ____________   Afternoon ____________   Evening ____________

Physical Movement

Walking, Yoga, Running, Weight lifting, Stretching, Jiu Jitsu, Pilates, or another: ____________

Resistance (Tasks for the Day)

Creative ____

Professional ____

Relationship(s) ____

Self ____

Evening Review

How did it go? What lesson(s) did I learn? Who do I need to make an amends with or forgive?

____

____

Mod 3 // Day 2

Reading

We are not of the body. We are of the spirit. Another way to say this comes from *A Course in Miracles*, which says: "I am not a body. I am free. For I am still as God created me." (Lesson 201) It's when we forget that we are of the spirit that we shift out of the witness and have forgotten who we are. We get lost in the drama. It's like we forget that we are an actor playing a character role, forgetting that we are not—and don't have to be—caught up in the role. In the amazing documentary *Jim and Andy: The Great Beyond*, the film documents Jim Carrey playing the role of Andy Kaufman for the movie *Man on the Moon*. The documentary was filmed alongside the movie, capturing Jim being fully in Andy's character—so much so that he fully commits to it in his daily life through the entire film. He was so connected to Andy that towards the end of the film, Andy's family came on set. And when Jim, as Andy, talked to them, they were shocked. It felt like they were talking to Andy. And then Jim, as Andy, said things to them that only Andy could have known. How could this be explained? Other than there is clearly a spiritual element happening.

And if we are to continue to live from that place of love, light, and truth, then we are far more available to access knowledge and wisdom than what our finite minds can comprehend. Being of the Spirit opens us up beyond the local conscious body to the collective consciousness. Then we are back to being connected to Source and not limited to the ego's roles and separation it tries to continue to cast as real. What if Jim's channeling of Andy is and was more real than the roles we live from day to day? What if Jim's performance was more honest because he knew what he was doing? For us, if we often don't know that we're in the role, and whose role are we playing? Could it be that we aren't being honest with ourselves? When you know you're playing a role, you have freedom. You can step in and out of it. You can choose it consciously. You can serve the story without being consumed by it. But when you forget you're playing a role—when you think the character *is* you—you're trapped. You've lost yourself in the drama. This is what it means to forget you are Spirit. You become identified with the role—the job title, the relationship status, the social persona, the wounded story, the smaller self. Remember the witness. Remember who you really are.

Journaling

What am I believing and experiencing today (emotionally, physically and spiritually)? What is my positive mindset and my negative mindset? How can I reparent myself with my current situation? What would the voice of Love say?

____

____

____

____

____

Vision

Reconnect to your Vision // What structure and implemenation needs to occur today?

____

____

Meditation

Dawnos *Oriented* Album // Track 8 – Sourcing

Affirmation

Morning Affirmation _______________________________   Evening Affirmation _______________________________

Pausing   (Write out the times // set alarms)

Morning _____________   Midday _____________   Afternoon _____________   Evening _____________

Physical Movement

Walking, Yoga, Running, Weight lifting, Stretching, Jiu Jitsu, Pilates, or another: _______________

Resistance (Tasks for the Day)

Creative ____

Professional ____

Relationship(s) ____

Self ____

Evening Review

How did it go? What lesson(s) did I learn? Who do I need to make an amends with or forgive?

____

____

____

Mod 3 // Day 3

Reading

We are all mirrors, reflecting either positive light or negative shadows. Think of it this way: When you walk into a room and sense someone's anger or anxiety, that exchange has already happened. Because you felt it. You sensed it. The same is true with someone who is joyful and happy. Laughter and anxiety are contagious. **This daily practice, the importance of our daily rhythm of "The Work," is to access the light within and send it out.** And also, when negative energy encounters us, we perform the alchemy—which means we process through it and exchange negativity for positivity. There are some days when we all wake up in a low mood and energy. We are just negative. These moments are crucial to access the light within. Maybe it's just an ember, and we breathe love back into it and fan the flame. So I invite you into a short exercise this morning. Think of a close friend who is or has been in a similar situation to where you are and what you are currently struggling with. Then write out very clearly and concisely what you want this person to know about themselves and what's possible for them—how they can grow and expand. Address this friend's shame, fear, and moments of doubt. What would you tell them? **[Stop here and write it out before you read the next paragraph.]**

Have you ever heard the phrase "you spot it, you got it"? This phrase is often given as a caution when we are judging others—which is true, because the very thoughts and feelings we have for another are mirroring something inside us. We wouldn't be thinking it or feeling it if we somehow didn't have that very thing within us. But in this practice, the positive is also true. Take your time and allow yourself to reflect on the positive words you have said to your friend, and allow them to soak into your being and soul. We all need a massive amount of light and encouragement. Allow this to inspire you for the rest of the day. What you just wrote for your friend? That's also for you. The encouragement you offered them, the hope you spoke over them, the truth you reminded them of—you need to hear it too. So today, carry those words with you. Not just for your friend, but for yourself. You are worthy of the same encouragement, the same hope, the same belief.

Journaling

What am I believing and experiencing today (emotionally, physically and spiritually)? What is my positive mindset and my negative mindset? How can I reparent myself with my current situation? What would the voice of Love say?

____

____

____

____

____

Vision

Reconnect to your Vision // What structure and implemenation needs to occur today?

____

____

Meditation

Dawnos _Oriented_ Album // Track 9 - Healing Light

Affirmation

Morning Affirmation ______________________________   Evening Affirmation ______________________________

Pausing (Write out the times // set alarms)

Morning ______________   Midday ______________   Afternoon ______________   Evening ______________

Physical Movement

Walking, Yoga, Running, Weight lifting, Stretching, Jiu Jitsu, Pilates, or another: ______________

Resistance (Tasks for the Day)

Creative ____

Professional ____

Relationship(s) ____

Self ____

Evening Review

How did it go? What lesson(s) did I learn? Who do I need to make an amends with or forgive?

____

____

____

Mod 3 // Day 4

Reading

The desire to know, to have certainty, is deeply human—and it is also the trap. The need for certainty is the ego's way of maintaining control, rather than learning to live by faith. As you have committed to this curriculum—to the daily rhythm of doing "the work"—by this point you likely have a vision. That vision may be broad, or it may be very specific. For some, it looks like returning to graduate school, in order to pursue a particular profession. For others, the vision is less about a role or title and more about a way of living—being more present, serving your community, showing up differently for your spouse and your children, and living from a deeper place of integrity and care. Whatever form your vision takes, the invitation here is not to force knowing, but to hold that vision close to your heart while you practice embracing the unknown.

This is where the SOURCE tool becomes especially helpful as a lived practice and a support. **S — Seek.** Ask God, Source, or your higher power for aid and guidance. **O — Open.** Allow yourself to be open to wisdom and direction that exists beyond your finite knowledge and limited understanding. **U — Unknown.** Invite in not knowing. Let yourself feel it rather than rushing past it. **R — Resource.** Bring to mind mentors, guides, or people who love you. Imagine what your highest, older, wiser self might say to you in this moment. **C — Compassion.** Allow yourself to receive the encouragement, care, and reassurance that arise as you hold your vision gently. **E — Experience.** Notice the thoughts, emotions, sensations, and qualities of what is happening, and practice being with whatever arises without needing to change it.

Finally, consider this, faith is learning to trust what you sense before you can see it. Let this be something you hold and return to. As the ego mind grasps for certainty, notice that impulse. Instead of living from certainty, practice living from faith—today, in this very moment, exactly as it is.

Journaling

What am I believing and experiencing today (emotionally, physically and spiritually)? What is my positive mindset and my negative mindset? How can I reparent myself with my current situation? What would the voice of Love say?

____

____

____

____

____

____

Vision

Reconnect to your Vision // What structure and implemenation needs to occur today?

____

____

Meditation

Dawnos *Oriented* Album // Track 7 - SOURCE

Affirmation

Morning Affirmation _______________________   Evening Affirmation _______________________

Pausing   (Write out the times // set alarms)

Morning _____________   Midday _____________   Afternoon _____________   Evening _____________

Physical Movement

Walking, Yoga, Running, Weight lifting, Stretching, Jiu Jitsu, Pilates, or another: _______________

Resistance (Tasks for the Day)

Creative ____

Professional ____

Relationship(s) ____

Self ____

Evening Review

How did it go? What lesson(s) did I learn? Who do I need to make an amends with or forgive?

____

____

____

Mod 3 // Day 5

Reading

Loving yourself can feel like an awkward concept. Most of us don't talk this way. But this is the truth: how we relate to ourselves is how we relate to the world. The love—or lack of love—we offer ourselves becomes the template for every relationship, every interaction, every moment of our lives.

The first question is simple, but deeply revealing: **Do you love yourself?** This matters because if you don't love yourself, how can you tend to yourself? How can you offer care, patience, and gentleness to your own process? And there's something else here that's important to notice: if you're not open to loving yourself, you will also block love coming from others. Even when people are genuinely trying to love you, support you, or care for you, it can't fully land if you're closed to it within yourself. Sit with this honestly—not conceptually, but experientially. Do you actually love yourself?

The second question builds on this: **Are you encouraging yourself and believing in yourself through your own process?** And just as important—are you open to being encouraged? If you're unwilling to encourage yourself or hold faith in yourself, you'll often block encouragement coming from others as well.

The third question returns us to something even larger: **Do you feel that the universe—God, Source, your higher power—is working on your behalf?** Do you sense that there is care for you, not against you? That you are actually being held, guided, and supported—even when life feels difficult or unclear?

These three questions reveal something essential. They show us where we are open and where we are blocked. And that is the work—not fixing, not forcing, but noticing. Examining. Allowing ourselves to be gently challenged by what we discover. Take these questions with you today. Sit with them. When you're unsure, notice how you would respond to your own child—and pause there.

Journaling

What am I believing and experiencing today (emotionally, physically and spiritually)? What is my positive mindset and my negative mindset? How can I reparent myself with my current situation? What would the voice of Love say?

____

____

____

____

____

Vision

Reconnect to your Vision // What structure and implemenation needs to occur today?

____

____

Meditation

Dawnos _Air_ Album // Track 6 - Rhythm

Affirmation

Morning Affirmation ______________________________   Evening Affirmation ______________________________

Pausing (Write out the times // set alarms)

Morning ______________   Midday ______________   Afternoon ______________   Evening ______________

Physical Movement

Walking, Yoga, Running, Weight lifting, Stretching, Jiu Jitsu, Pilates, or another: ______________

Resistance (Tasks for the Day)

Creative ____

Professional ____

Relationship(s) ____

Self ____

Evening Review

How did it go? What lesson(s) did I learn? Who do I need to make an amends with or forgive?

____

____

Mod 3 // Day 6

Reading

There is, and remains, the ability—and the choice—to see the light instead of the darkness. And that choice is what enables the vision. This spiritual light is of another kind. It is hope. Love. Possibility. Courage. Forgiveness. Acceptance. Peace. It is what saves us from our problem—which is our old belief that we are separate and small, limited in our way of being. This Smaller Self, which we will explore more deeply in a later module, is saved—if you will—by remembering and bringing forth this light of Source.

This is where the practice of "sourcing" becomes so important. What this means is meditating on this inner light of awareness—and recognizing that we have a part in this: the light being turned back on. The good news is that safety, promise, and wholeness are available now. It simply requires us to be open and available to see and hear differently. Today's practice is about doing this very thing—not only seeing and hearing, but allowing yourself to feel, on a deeper conscious level, this love, abundance, and peace. By this, we turn on the light.

So today, take time to meditate on the inner light—not only as a metaphor, but as an actual state of mind. **We do have the power of choice: to see light instead of darkness, love instead of fear. This is not a denial of reality, but an acceptance of Reality as it is.** From that place, we are able to bring light and love to a situation, rather than fear, separation, and reactivity. As Thomas Merton sums it up so well, *"We are already one. But we imagine that we are not."*

Journaling

What am I believing and experiencing today (emotionally, physically and spiritually)? What is my positive mindset and my negative mindset? How can I reparent myself with my current situation? What would the voice of Love say?

____

____

____

____

____

____

____

Vision

Reconnect to your Vision // What structure and implemenation needs to occur today?

____

____

Meditation

Dawnos *Oriented* Album // Track 8 - Sourcing

Affirmation

Morning Affirmation ___________________________   Evening Affirmation ___________________________

Pausing (Write out the times // set alarms)

Morning ____________   Midday ____________   Afternoon ____________   Evening ____________

Physical Movement

Walking, Yoga, Running, Weight lifting, Stretching, Jiu Jitsu, Pilates, or another: _______________

Resistance (Tasks for the Day)

Creative ____

Professional ____

Relationship(s) ____

Self ____

Evening Review

How did it go? What lesson(s) did I learn? Who do I need to make an amends with or forgive?

____

____

____

Mod 3 // Day 7

Reading

Something profound occurs when we connect and reorient. When we do, we establish our path—or more accurately, our path establishes us—for the purpose of love: to be loved, to love, and to be loving. I don't want to assume this has been your experience, but for a long time, whenever I heard messages about love, they felt obvious—and landed flat. Of course we're supposed to love. It didn't feel new or particularly transformative. But what I've learned is this: when I truly allow that truth in, **love never leads me astray. It does not fail.** In fact, it's the only way to live—and at times, it feels surprisingly radical.

I want you to pause and consider a recent moment of tension—an argument, a frustration, a moment of fear. Imagine yourself saying to the other person, *It's okay.* And depending on the situation, imagine saying—either internally or out loud—*I love you.* This is anything but soft or sentimental. It requires a deep and radical devotion to hold steady in love rather than react from fear.

Just yesterday, I found myself in a familiar argument with a family member—one that has happened before. I stepped outside and took a short walk. What became clear was simple and demanding at the same time: I needed to love them. I chose, in that moment, to ask Love for its wisdom—to guide me when I went back inside. And it did. I was able to take full responsibility for my part, reconnect, and return to the relationship.

And don't forget—often the one who needs just as much love is you. That's why that phrase begins with *loved, love, loving*—which can also be understood as *receive, be, and give.*

Journaling

What am I believing and experiencing today (emotionally, physically and spiritually)? What is my positive mindset and my negative mindset? How can I reparent myself with my current situation? What would the voice of Love say?

____

____

____

____

____

____

____

Vision

Reconnect to your Vision // What structure and implemenation needs to occur today?

____

____

Meditation

Dawnos *Air* Album // Track 3 - Fire Breath

Affirmation

Morning Affirmation ______________________________   Evening Affirmation ________________________________

Pausing   (Write out the times // set alarms)

Morning ____________   Midday ____________   Afternoon ____________   Evening ____________

Physical Movement

Walking, Yoga, Running, Weight lifting, Stretching, Jiu Jitsu, Pilates, or another: ______________

Resistance (Tasks for the Day)

Creative ____

Professional ____

Relationship(s) ____

Self ____

Evening Review

How did it go? What lesson(s) did I learn? Who do I need to make an amends with or forgive?

____

____

Four

Body

The body is the vessel—the capsule that carries your life, your soul, your calling. **Whether we realize it or not, we are always in relationship with it. Either we are serving the body, or the body is serving us.** When we serve the body, we live at the mercy of its urges and reactions. We follow appetite, impulse, comfort, and avoidance. We chase relief. We numb. We react. This happens not because the body is bad, but because we've over-identified with it. We've mistaken the vessel for the one who inhabits it. We say, *I am anxious. I am tired. I am restless.* Slowly, the body becomes the master. But this is not the relationship we're meant to live from.

We are not the body. And at the same time, the body is an essential part of us. This distinction matters. When we learn to form practices that return us to the seat of awareness—where the body serves rather than rules—we access a larger state of maturity and freedom. Developmentally, this is the natural arc of growth. As children, we live almost entirely from bodily impulse. Hunger, fatigue, desire, discomfort—these signals run the show. Over time, we are meant to grow beyond this elementary state, not by rejecting the body, but by learning how to work with it.

The body is not something to be conquered or despised. It is an intelligent, responsive instrument. It signals when something is off. It responds to truth and reacts to falsehood. It stores unresolved experience and expresses joy with ease. It carries memory, trauma, instinct, and intuition. This is why we so often speak from the body without realizing it: *My gut says no. That doesn't sit right. Something feels off.* We intuitively know what science now confirms—that the gut functions as a kind of second brain, processing information beneath conscious thought and signaling safety or threat. The body is always speaking. The problem is not that the body speaks—it's that we either ignore it or become ruled by it.

In this module, you'll learn a third way: how to live in right relationship with your body. You'll learn how to engage it, listen to it, and honor it—without over-identifying with it. You'll begin to notice sensation without becoming it. You'll learn how to ground yourself, shift physical states, work with energy, and rest in a way that actually restores. Not by escaping the body, and not by indulging it, but by partnering with it. As you move through this week, your invited to reflect on these questions: Where are you serving your body out of compulsion or avoidance? Where are you ignoring its wisdom? And where might you begin to engage it as an ally in your life and work? This is the work here. Not rejecting the body. Not being enslaved by it. But learning to live in right relationship with it. Your body is a gift—an instrument finely tuned to help you navigate this life and fulfill your purpose. When you learn to listen without surrendering your seat, the body becomes what it was always meant to be: a trusted partner in the sacred work you're here to do.

Mod 4 // Day 1

Reading

Here is a simple truth that can feel like a contradiction: you are meant to fully inhabit your body, but you are not your body. You have a purpose—one that gives your life meaning and direction. Your joy flows from fulfilling it. Your body is the vessel designed to help you do exactly that. It is not your identity; it is your vehicle. Understanding this relationship is a major developmental step. Early in life, we live almost entirely from the body—hunger, fatigue, comfort, pleasure, and pain shape our decisions. This is natural. As we grow, the body moves through distinct phases of development. In adolescence, that process reaches a new level of intensity and self-awareness, and identity often becomes entangled with appearance, performance, and comparison. Again, this is not wrong—it is a stage. But if development stops here, the body begins to carry more authority than it was meant to hold.

When identity collapses into the body, something subtle happens. Sensation becomes self. Emotion becomes truth. We say, *I am anxious, I am exhausted, I am restless.* **Without realizing it, the body becomes the master.** Not because it is bad or untrustworthy, but because it was never meant to lead alone. **Maturity does not come from rejecting the body. It comes from restoring order.** When awareness takes its rightful seat, the body relaxes into partnership. Health becomes about vitality rather than control. Beauty becomes an expression of joy rather than a measure of worth. Something softens when the body is no longer asked to answer questions it cannot answer—questions of identity, meaning, and belonging. The gift is this: you don't have to wait until old age to arrive here. You don't have to deny desire or discipline the body into submission. You simply learn to relate differently. The body becomes an instrument rather than an authority, a servant to your calling rather than the source of your value.

This week is about restoring that relationship. Not distancing from the body, and not surrendering to it—but learning to live from awareness while fully inhabiting your physical life. This is where freedom begins.

Journaling

What am I believing and experiencing today (emotionally, physically and spiritually)? What is my positive mindset and my negative mindset? How can I reparent myself with my current situation? What would the voice of Love say?

____

____

____

____

____

____

Vision

Reconnect to your Vision // What structure and implemenation needs to occur today?

____

____

Meditation

Dawnos *Oriented* Album // Track 10 – Felt Sense

Affirmation

Morning Affirmation _______________________   Evening Affirmation _______________________

Pausing   (Write out the times // set alarms)

Morning _____________   Midday _____________   Afternoon _____________   Evening _____________

Physical Movement

Walking, Yoga, Running, Weight lifting, Stretching, Jiu Jitsu, Pilates, or another: _______________

Resistance (Tasks for the Day)

Creative ____

Professional ____

Relationship(s) ____

Self ____

Evening Review

How did it go? What lesson(s) did I learn? Who do I need to make an amends with or forgive?

____

____

____

Mod 4 // Day 2

Reading

Rest can be deceptive. We often seek it hoping for peace, relief from anxiety, or escape from mental noise. While physical rest is essential, not all rest restores. There is a shadow side to rest that is easy to miss—one that pulls us toward collapse rather than integration. When the nervous system has been activated for too long, the body looks for relief. This activation belongs to the sympathetic nervous system—the part of us designed for action, urgency, and protection. When it never fully powers down, the system becomes exhausted. In response, we may numb out through distraction, dissociation, or endless consumption. This can feel restful in the moment, but it doesn't restore. It suspends.

True rest belongs to the parasympathetic state—the condition of safety where digestion improves, breath slows, and the body no longer needs to brace. This kind of rest cannot be forced. It emerges naturally when the system feels met. Presence, not avoidance, is what invites it. This is why emotional and cognitive rest matter as much as physical rest. Simply stopping activity does not quiet a racing mind or an anxious body. What calms the system is attention—gentle, curious, and non-judging. **When you stay with physical sensation rather than escaping it, energy that was held in vigilance begins to settle and transform.**

Rest comes after listening. After the body knows it doesn't have to keep signaling. When awareness turns toward experience instead of away from it, the system receives the message it has been waiting for: *you are safe enough right now*. Today is about letting everything land. There is nothing to accomplish and nothing to fix. Simply notice where your body is holding tension. Feel the breath. Sense contact with the ground. Allow the body to settle in its own time. This is not collapse. It is integration. And from here, rest arrives and is restorative.

Journaling

What am I believing and experiencing today (emotionally, physically and spiritually)? What is my positive mindset and my negative mindset? How can I reparent myself with my current situation? What would the voice of Love say?

Vision

Reconnect to your Vision // What structure and implemenation needs to occur today?

____

____

Meditation

Dawnos _Air_ Album // Track 4 – Expansion

Affirmation

Morning Affirmation _______________________________   Evening Affirmation _______________________________

Pausing   (Write out the times // set alarms)

Morning _____________   Midday _____________   Afternoon _____________   Evening _____________

Physical Movement

Walking, Yoga, Running, Weight lifting, Stretching, Jiu Jitsu, Pilates, or another: _______________

Resistance (Tasks for the Day)

Creative ____

Professional ____

Relationship(s) ____

Self ____

Evening Review

How did it go? What lesson(s) did I learn? Who do I need to make an amends with or forgive?

____

____

____

Mod 4 // Day 3

Reading

As you reconnect with your body, you will naturally encounter sensation—tension, fatigue, emotion, discomfort. Nothing has gone wrong. This is awareness returning. What we avoid doesn't disappear; it waits. When attention comes back, the body speaks again. What is often overlooked is that you have agency within these states. Many of us believe we are trapped by how we feel physically, but the body is far more responsive than we realize. While you may not control what arises, you can learn how to work with it. This is where behavior often gets misunderstood. **When we are disconnected from the body, the body becomes the driver. We then fixate on habits—restlessness, procrastination, numbing—trying to correct behavior without listening beneath it.** But behavior is rarely the root issue. It is the body's attempt to regulate energy, stress, or emotion.

Movement plays a critical role here. When the sympathetic nervous system (fight, flight, freeze, fawn) is activated, energy builds. If that energy has nowhere to go, it turns inward—into anxiety, irritability, or mental noise. Gentle movement allows the body to complete stress cycles. Walking, stretching, shaking, or intentional exercise helps discharge activation and restore balance. This is why movement is essential for mental well-being. Not as discipline or optimization, but as regulation. Dopamine supports motivation and hope. Endorphins buffer emotional dips. The body feels better because it *is* better regulated. When you respond to your body with curiosity instead of frustration, it often tells you exactly what it needs. Small adjustments—posture, breath, movement—can shift an entire internal state. The body is not something to endure. It is something you can cooperate with.

Journaling

What am I believing and experiencing today (emotionally, physically and spiritually)? What is my positive mindset and my negative mindset? How can I reparent myself with my current situation? What would the voice of Love say?

____

____

____

____

____

____

____

Vision

Reconnect to your Vision // What structure and implemenation needs to occur today?

____

____

Meditation

Dawnos *Oriented* Album // Track 12 – Energy Grid

Affirmation

Morning Affirmation ________________________________   Evening Affirmation ________________________________

Pausing   (Write out the times // set alarms)

Morning ______________   Midday ______________   Afternoon ______________   Evening ______________

Physical Movement

Walking, Yoga, Running, Weight lifting, Stretching, Jiu Jitsu, Pilates, or another: ______________

Resistance (Tasks for the Day)

Creative ____

Professional ____

Relationship(s) ____

Self ____

Evening Review

How did it go? What lesson(s) did I learn? Who do I need to make an amends with or forgive?

____

____

Mod 4 // Day 4

Reading

One of the most powerful shifts you can make is learning to observe bodily experience rather than reacting from the initial waves of unprocessed energy. When we say, *I am anxious* or *I am in pain*, identity collapses into sensation. Awareness disappears into experience, and the mind fills in the rest—often with stories, predictions, and assumptions that feel real but are not actually happening now. The Felt Sense practice invites a different posture. Instead of merging with sensation or trying to think your way through it, you notice it. You ask simple, grounding questions: *Where do I feel this in my body?* Is it tight or heavy? Does it have a temperature, a texture, a shape? As attention moves into sensation, something important happens—rumination begins to loosen. **The ruminating mind tends to project a false reality. It replays the past or rehearses the future and then reacts as if that imagined scenario is present. By bringing attention into the body, you interrupt this loop. You return from story to sensation. From projection to contact.** From imagined threat to actual experience. Additional questions can deepen this process: *If this sensation had a color, what would it be? If it had an age, how old does it feel?* These questions are not meant to analyze or interpret. They gently bypass the thinking mind and invite a more intuitive, embodied awareness to emerge. The body responds to metaphor and image more readily than logic.

As you stay with the Felt Sense, space opens between awareness and sensation. You can feel anxiety without being consumed by it. You can notice discomfort without letting it define your entire experience. The body is honored, but it no longer runs the show. Over time, sensations lose their grip—not because they are suppressed, but because they are seen. Breathwork supports this shift. Slow, intentional breathing—especially extended exhales—signals safety to the nervous system and helps anchor awareness in the present moment. Breath, sensation, and awareness begin to work together. This is how false reality dissolves—not through positive thinking or control, but through contact. Awareness returns to what is actually here. And from that place, clarity naturally follows.

Journaling

What am I believing and experiencing today (emotionally, physically and spiritually)? What is my positive mindset and my negative mindset? How can I reparent myself with my current situation? What would the voice of Love say?

____

____

____

____

____

____

Vision

Reconnect to your Vision // What structure and implemenation needs to occur today?

____

____

Meditation

Dawnos *Oriented* Album // Track 10 – Felt Sense

Affirmation

Morning Affirmation ______________________________   Evening Affirmation ______________________________

Pausing   (Write out the times // set alarms)

Morning ______________   Midday ______________   Afternoon ______________   Evening ______________

Physical Movement

Walking, Yoga, Running, Weight lifting, Stretching, Jiu Jitsu, Pilates, or another: ______________

Resistance (Tasks for the Day)

Creative ____

Professional ____

Relationship(s) ____

Self ____

Evening Review

How did it go? What lesson(s) did I learn? Who do I need to make an amends with or forgive?

____

____

Mod 4 // Day 5

Reading

Grounding is about orientation. It answers a simple but essential question: *Where am I right now?* Before working with emotion, memory, or energy, the nervous system needs contact—feet on the floor, weight in the body, breath moving slowly. Grounding is not about fixing or changing anything. It is about arriving back to presence. **When you are grounded, awareness lands. The body begins to feel less like a threat and more like a home.** There is a sense of being located—here, now, in this moment. Without grounding, attention tends to *float* upward into thought, story, and imagination. With grounding, awareness *settles* into actual experience.

This is why, in The Holland Method, we often ask a simple question: *Where do you feel it in your body?* This question is not diagnostic or analytical. It gently moves attention out of abstraction and into sensation. Much of our suffering is not caused by what is happening, but by what the mind is projecting—replaying the past or rehearsing the future and reacting as if it is happening now. When attention moves into the body, that projection begins to dissolve. Sensation only exists in the present moment. By locating experience physically, you step out of rumination and back into reality.

From here, additional Felt Sense questions may arise naturally: *What's the quality of the sensation—tight, heavy, warm, buzzing? If it had a color, what would it be? If it had an age, how old does it feel?* These questions are not meant to figure anything out. They gently bypass the thinking mind and invite a more intuitive awareness to emerge. The body responds to image and metaphor more readily than logic. As you stay with the Felt Sense, something settles. The nervous system receives a signal of safety. Awareness is no longer chasing meaning; it is making contact. Often, intensity softens—not because it is forced to change, but because it is finally being met. **Grounding establishes orientation. The Felt Sense deepens relationship. Together, they restore contact with what is real.** Today's practice is simple: feel the ground, notice the breath, and when something arises, ask gently—*where do I feel this in my body?* Then stay with it!

Journaling

What am I believing and experiencing today (emotionally, physically and spiritually)? What is my positive mindset and my negative mindset? How can I reparent myself with my current situation? What would the voice of Love say?

____

____

____

____

____

Vision

Reconnect to your Vision // What structure and implemenation needs to occur today?

____

____

Meditation

Dawnos *Oriented* Album // Track 11 – Grounding

Affirmation

Morning Affirmation _______________________   Evening Affirmation _______________________

Pausing   (Write out the times // set alarms)

Morning _____________   Midday _____________   Afternoon _____________   Evening _____________

Physical Movement

Walking, Yoga, Running, Weight lifting, Stretching, Jiu Jitsu, Pilates, or another: _______________

Resistance (Tasks for the Day)

Creative ____

Professional ____

Relationship(s) ____

Self ____

Evening Review

How did it go? What lesson(s) did I learn? Who do I need to make an amends with or forgive?

____

____

Mod 4 // Day 6

Reading

Energy is always moving through the body—as emotion, activation, vitality, or tension. Difficulty does not come from energy itself, but from how we relate to it. Most of us were never taught how to work with energy, only how to suppress it, distract from it, or amplify it through reaction. **When energy is resisted, it becomes emotional congested. When it is indulged or fueled by story, it overwhelms.** But when it is witnessed with awareness, it naturally completes its cycle. The body knows how to do this. It has always known. Much of what we experience as anxiety, restlessness, or emotional intensity is simply uncompleted energy—often linked to sympathetic nervous system activation. The system is mobilized, but the energy has nowhere to go. Instead of resolving, it loops. This is not a personal failure; it is a physiological reality.

Breath plays a central role here. The breath is one of the most direct regulators of the nervous system. When breath is shallow, held, or restricted, energy becomes trapped. When breath is slow, full, and unforced—especially with longer exhales—it signals safety and allows energy to move. Breath does not eliminate sensation; it creates space for it. Movement, grounding, and breath all work together. **Movement helps discharge activation. Grounding provides containment.** Breath allows energy to rise, crest, and fall without interference. You are not trying to control the process, only accompany it.

As you stay present, energy begins to change on its own. What once felt overwhelming becomes workable. What felt threatening becomes information. Over time, the body learns that it does not need to brace against its own experience. Energy is not the enemy. It is simply movement asking to be acknowledged. When awareness meets it—without resistance or indulgence—the body remembers how to regulate itself. This is not something you force. It is something you allow. Today, notice energy as movement rather than meaning. Stay with breath. Stay with sensation. Let the body do what it knows how to do. Completion happens quietly, when awareness is willing to stay.

Journaling

What am I believing and experiencing today (emotionally, physically and spiritually)? What is my positive mindset and my negative mindset? How can I reparent myself with my current situation? What would the voice of Love say?

____

____

____

____

____

Vision

Reconnect to your Vision // What structure and implemenation needs to occur today?

____

____

Meditation

Dawnos _Air_ Album // Track 2 – Downshift

Affirmation

Morning Affirmation ______________________________   Evening Affirmation ______________________________

Pausing   (Write out the times // set alarms)

Morning ____________   Midday ____________   Afternoon ____________   Evening ____________

Physical Movement

Walking, Yoga, Running, Weight lifting, Stretching, Jiu Jitsu, Pilates, or another: ______________

Resistance (Tasks for the Day)

Creative ____

Professional ____

Relationship(s) ____

Self ____

Evening Review

How did it go? What lesson(s) did I learn? Who do I need to make an amends with or forgive?

____

____

Mod 4 // Day 7

Reading

We all know these moments—times when the body is suddenly flooded with intense energy: anxiety, panic, depression. This is simply part of living this life. The journey isn't to eliminate these experiences, but to learn how to be with the energy itself—to acclimate to it, to work with it, and to allow it to move and eventually dissolve. It's all a practice.

This is why practices like cold plunge therapy can be so beneficial—not only for their physical effects, such as reducing inflammation, but for the emotional and nervous-system training happening underneath. You are choosing discomfort. You are meeting intensity on purpose. Rather than resisting the energy, you invite it in with awareness. And in doing so, what once felt overwhelming begins to transform.

The incredible gift of having tools—such as breathwork practices, the felt sense, and other grounding techniques—is that they interrupt the illusion that we are trapped in our own bodies, forced to endure whatever state we happen to be in as if it were a cage. What once felt like helplessness becomes workable. We can be with sensation. We can engage it directly, with curiosity—looking right at it, observing it. This is strength.

Awareness is what makes this possible. It is the living link between body and soul. When we rest there, we return to the seat of consciousness—we wake up. Awake to whatever human experience, feeling, or emotion arises. These states are not failures; they are part of inhabiting a body. But instead of being subject to their seemingly fateful, wild waves, we learn to ride them—no longer as victims, but as present, grounded observers, masters of our own inner domain.

Journaling

What am I believing and experiencing today (emotionally, physically and spiritually)? What is my positive mindset and my negative mindset? How can I reparent myself with my current situation? What would the voice of Love say?

Vision

Reconnect to your Vision // What structure and implemenation needs to occur today?

____

____

Meditation

Dawnos *Air* Album // Track 3 – Fire Breath

Affirmation

Morning Affirmation ______________________________   Evening Affirmation ______________________________

Pausing (Write out the times // set alarms)

Morning ____________   Midday ____________   Afternoon ____________   Evening ____________

Physical Movement

Walking, Yoga, Running, Weight lifting, Stretching, Jiu Jitsu, Pilates, or another: ______________

Resistance (Tasks for the Day)

Creative ____

Professional ____

Relationship(s) ____

Self ____

Evening Review

How did it go? What lesson(s) did I learn? Who do I need to make an amends with or forgive?

____

____

Notes:

Five

Thoughts

Success, love, accomplishment, peace, wholeness—it's all a mindset. Years ago, I was averse to this type of 'mindset' thinking, oddly enough. I felt like it was more of a performative, success-oriented, American idea. And in my mind, I'd picture some guy on stage trying to sell his motivational book on sales or empowerment, all of that. The irony is, there are great truths and tenets to much of those types of books—provided they are linked to a higher & true self calling, not the ego calling. So as it relates to mindset: **What we think is what we project. And what we project, we see as real.** The problem is that our perceptions are often misguided and not based on reality. You may question this? I know I did. Just sit with a married couple who is in an argument and try to determine who is right or wrong. It is incredibly challenging and confusing. Both are partially correct, at least from their side. But here's the catch and key: While someone might be "right" in their eyes, if it's from a spirit of "being right", then they have unconsciously "othered" themselves and created separation instead of connection. Therefore, it's of the ego mind. From a mind of Love, we seek to understand, connect, and remain open with curiosity. Or think how fear casts such a shadow on pursuing your dream, especially when it comes to finances. Immediately, the inner critic creates a narrative of "you can't" or a rational reason why "you shouldn't" do it. And if you move forward with the vision, that inner critic will even get louder.

This is where we need some very important tools to help through this stage. The good news is that just as easily as it is to hear the inner critic, we can hear the inner loving parent too. It just takes tuning in and being open. We have the power to choose our thoughts. We can choose to 'think' differently. It only requires some intention and training, which is why daily affirmations are so vital to the whole process and practice. And that is what this next module will walk you through. **Your mindset isn't about forcing positivity or pretending everything is fine. It's about recognizing that you have a choice in how you interpret what's happening.** You can see through the lens of fear or the lens of love. You can listen to the inner critic or the inner loving parent. Both voices are there. Both are speaking. The question is: which one will you tune into? The mind of fear says: You can't. You shouldn't. You're not enough. It won't work. The mind of Love says: You are capable. You are worthy. You are supported. Trust the process. Both mindsets create a reality. Both project outward and shape what you experience. The difference is, one keeps you small and separate. The other opens you to expansion, possibility, and connection. So the work—the practice—is learning to shift from one to the other. Not once, but daily. Not perfectly, but intentionally. This is what the next module will teach you. Not motivational hype, but practical tools rooted in truth and love. You have the power to choose your thoughts and shift your mindset. And when you do, everything changes.

Reading

A process that has helped me immensely when I'm caught in confusion, stress, or despair—or even when I simply need to gather myself—is The Questions Tool. This is often the first place I go when I need clarity. It doesn't require being in crisis or doing deep emotional work. I return to it because I need to settle in, slow down, and re-orient. When the mind feels noisy or foggy, this tool helps me get centered again. At its heart, The Questions Tool brings us back to a different state of mind: the **mind of Love**. It helps us learn to see and hear from connection rather than from fear. The mind of fear belongs to the ego and creates separation; the mind of Love restores connection.

The Questions are simple, but they're powerful: 1) **"Am I open to seeing or hearing this differently?"** This question opens the door to a new perspective—one beyond the story you've been locked into. 2) **"Is this the mind of fear or the mind of Love?"** This is an orientation question. It helps you honestly assess where your thinking is coming from. 3) **"Am I willing to be in the care of Love?"** Instead of framing this as surrender, what if it's about nurture? Letting go doesn't have to be forceful or hard. 4) **"What happens when I listen to or see from the mind of fear?"** When you believe fear, notice how you think, react, and respond. This question helps you recognize fear's patterns and signals. 5) **"What does the mind of Love say or show?"** This is where peace enters. The message that arises here is what guides, directs, and restores connection. And here's the key: Our only job—our only task—is to be open, notice, and receive.

Journaling

What am I believing and experiencing today (emotionally, physically and spiritually)? What is my positive mindset and my negative mindset? How can I reparent myself with my current situation? What would the voice of Love say?

____

____

____

____

____

____

____

____

Vision

Reconnect to your Vision // What structure and implemenation needs to occur today?

____

____

Meditation

Dawnos _Disoriented_ Album // Track 1 – The Questions

Affirmation

Morning Affirmation ______________________________   Evening Affirmation __________________________________

Pausing   (Write out the times // set alarms)

Morning _____________   Midday _____________   Afternoon _____________   Evening _____________

Physical Movement

Walking, Yoga, Running, Weight lifting, Stretching, Jiu Jitsu, Pilates, or another: _______________

Resistance (Tasks for the Day)

Creative ____

Professional ____

Relationship(s) ____

Self ____

Evening Review

How did it go? What lesson(s) did I learn? Who do I need to make an amends with or forgive?

____

____

Reading

The mind of fear creates a convincing state of hallucination that feels real and certain. The mind of Love is quieter, yet always available—provided I am open and willing to see the situation differently. There are many moments I can look back on now where, if I could speak to my younger self, I would simply say, *You don't have to worry. It's going to be okay.* The mind of fear robs me of the joys of the day.

The way through is less a formula and more a process. It begins with getting still, going inward, and—paradoxically—inviting the negative belief in with a willingness to see and hear the situation through the mind of Love. This isn't easy. Often the emotions intensify at first. But when I stay with it—breathing, asking whether this fear is actually true right now, and asking the Spirit for help and guidance—something shifts. **When I release my expectations of how things should unfold, a softer awareness of love begins to surround me.** Often there is that quiet, ever-present voice saying, *I've got you. Everything will be okay.*

Last night, I found myself building upsetting scenarios in my mind—running through worst-case outcomes, convinced something painful was about to happen. I tried to challenge the thoughts, but the fear felt overpowering. And then the situation passed. None of the feared projections occurred. In fact, the opposite happened. This morning, as I reflect, a few things are clear: it makes sense that this fear arose, because I was hurt in this area of my life years ago; sometimes these moments need to run their course; and this is an invitation to gentle inquiry—to recognize a wounded, younger part of me that is still asking for love.

Journaling

What am I believing and experiencing today (emotionally, physically and spiritually)? What is my positive mindset and my negative mindset? How can I reparent myself with my current situation? What would the voice of Love say?

____

____

____

____

____

____

____

Vision

Reconnect to your Vision // What structure and implemenation needs to occur today?

____

____

Meditation

Dawnos _Disoriented_ Album // Track 2 – Voice of Love

Affirmation

Morning Affirmation ______________________________   Evening Affirmation ______________________________

Pausing   (Write out the times // set alarms)

Morning _____________   Midday _____________   Afternoon _____________   Evening _____________

Physical Movement

Walking, Yoga, Running, Weight lifting, Stretching, Jiu Jitsu, Pilates, or another: _______________

Resistance (Tasks for the Day)

Creative ____

Professional ____

Relationship(s) ____

Self ____

Evening Review

How did it go? What lesson(s) did I learn? Who do I need to make an amends with or forgive?

____

____

Reading

Every day, and even every moment, we have a choice. We can choose love or fear. We can choose to not only accept what is right in front of us, but to engage it differently. It's like we have an opportunity to live a new way, right at that moment of choice. And when we fully step into a decision to love, a vibrancy for life occurs. You engage life with purpose. Isn't this the ultimate mission for all of us? **The common denominator for every person is to love.** And from that, we can get really creative. Because then there is purpose and meaning. You are no longer a victim to the world—you get to be responsible to it and for it. Choice is a habit. And we all have the power to choose to see and hear either the voice of Love or fear. Heaven or hell. Yes, there are challenges. And yes, in the moment, it can feel hard to take the narrow road. But what alternative is there? Nobody's going to live your life other than you. Why not live big, bold, and radical through each choice? Sometimes this way means to be still. To be quiet. To be forgiven, or forgiving. Or just to be. To be with what is.

Take a moment. Step back and reflect on this day in front of you. See if you can view it positively. Bring energy and purpose to it. You have a choice right now. Not later. Not when things get easier. Not when circumstances change. Right now. Will you choose love or fear? Will you engage this day with purpose or drift through it unconsciously? Will you see yourself as a victim of your circumstances or as someone who can respond with creativity and meaning? The choice is always yours. And the beautiful thing is, you get to choose again in the next moment. And the next. Each choice builds on the last. Each decision to love strengthens your capacity to love again. This is how we create and build a life. Not through one grand decision, but through a thousand small choices made with intention and purpose. So today, choose to engage your life with love. Choose to be responsible for the energy you bring. **Choose to see the day before you as an opportunity rather than an obligation. Nobody else can live your life. Nobody else can make these choices for you. So live big hearted.** Live bold. Live radically. One choice at a time.

Journaling

What am I believing and experiencing today (emotionally, physically and spiritually)? What is my positive mindset and my negative mindset? How can I reparent myself with my current situation? What would the voice of Love say?

____

____

____

____

____

Vision

Reconnect to your Vision // What structure and implemenation needs to occur today?

____

____

Meditation

Dawnos *Air* Album // Track 1 – Box Breath

Affirmation

Morning Affirmation ________________________________   Evening Affirmation ______________________________________

Pausing **(Write out the times // set alarms)**

Morning ______________   Midday ______________   Afternoon ______________   Evening ______________

Physical Movement

Walking, Yoga, Running, Weight lifting, Stretching, Jiu Jitsu, Pilates, or another: ________________

Resistance (Tasks for the Day)

Creative ____

Professional ____

Relationship(s) ____

Self ____

Evening Review

How did it go? What lesson(s) did I learn? Who do I need to make an amends with or forgive?

____

____

Mod 5 // Day 4

Reading

It becomes clear that when we doubt ourselves, we invite in darkness—separation, the mind of fear. Doubt itself isn't the problem; it's human to have fearful thoughts. What matters is that we don't give those thoughts residence in the soulful place within us. You wouldn't knowingly let a dangerous thief into your home, hand them the keys, and walk away. And yet this is often what we do with fear. Because fear is familiar—an old companion—we've allowed it to interrupt and lead rather than learning from it. The work isn't to cut fear off or cast it out, but to notice it without handing it authority. We learn to interpret rather than exile, treating each emotion or thought as an uninvited guest—acknowledged, understood, but not in charge.

When we are awake and alert, nothing can be taken. Awareness restores agency. You know who you're dealing with, and fear loses its power to steal the present moment. In fact, fear can become useful. We have the ability to work with the energy inside us instead of being overtaken by it. Rather than allowing fear to hijack the moment, we learn to reparent those frightened places—bringing them back to truth, back to what is actually real. This is how fear is transformed: not by suppression, but by presence.

This landed personally for me today. I woke up with fear—fear about the work in front of me, about writing and various creative projects. What if nothing comes of it? I didn't push it away. I journaled about it all and was honest. And clarity returned. My purpose remains simple and steady: to share what I am passionate about and an unlimited supply of energy comes available when we're connected to the voice of Love. I know that voice to be the core. I know it's real. And I want you to discover it too. This is my focus point—back to center.

Journaling

What am I believing and experiencing today (emotionally, physically and spiritually)? What is my positive mindset and my negative mindset? How can I reparent myself with my current situation? What would the voice of Love say?

____

____

____

____

____

____

____

Vision

Reconnect to your Vision // What structure and implemenation needs to occur today?

____

____

Meditation

Dawnos *Disoriented* Album // Track 3 - Focus Point

Affirmation

Morning Affirmation ___________________________   Evening Affirmation ___________________________________

Pausing   (Write out the times // set alarms)

Morning _____________   Midday _____________   Afternoon _____________   Evening _____________

Physical Movement

Walking, Yoga, Running, Weight lifting, Stretching, Jiu Jitsu, Pilates, or another: _______________

Resistance (Tasks for the Day)

Creative ____

Professional ____

Relationship(s) ____

Self ____

Evening Review

How did it go? What lesson(s) did I learn? Who do I need to make an amends with or forgive?

____

____

Mod 5 // Day 5

Reading

There is a goodness within us that is undeniable—and yet, it must be remembered. It can feel trite or overly simplistic to speak this way, but returning to the core of goodness, to love, is how we find our way home within ourselves. One of the most subtle and damaging patterns in our lives—especially in our marriages and in our relationships with our children—is that we forget where we began. We tend to encounter love most vividly at the beginnings and endings of life, as if it belongs only there. But it doesn't. When we fail to turn inward and reconnect, we remain lost, caught in the trance of egoic thinking. **The task is learning to see yourself clearly—to see yourself in truth. This begins with stillness. With grounding. With gently making your way through the clouds.** If life feels complicated, or if *you* feel complicated, it usually means you're caught inside it—entangled in thoughts and emotions, these metaphorical clouds. But when you truly see yourself, stripped of distortion, how could love not arise? The challenge is that when we're caught in the trance, even hearing this can fail to land. So what do we do?

I'll speak more about jiu-jitsu in a later module, but one fundamental principle applies here. In jiu-jitsu, you're taught to maintain your frame—keeping strong structure and alignment through your arms and legs. When your frame is intact, you reduce exposure and limit risk, making it difficult for your opponent to create space, slip in hooks, or advance position. The moment structure collapses, leverage shifts. It's no different with our thoughts. Our daily work is awareness—maintaining a framed mindset. **Where we place our attention matters. Where our thoughts go, our behavior—and ultimately our life—follows. Our mindset is a choice.** And we can choose, again and again, to live from a mind rooted in love. So the question isn't whether love is available. It's simple—and difficult: will you choose it today?

Journaling

What am I believing and experiencing today (emotionally, physically and spiritually)? What is my positive mindset and my negative mindset? How can I reparent myself with my current situation? What would the voice of Love say?

____

____

____

____

____

____

Vision

Reconnect to your Vision // What structure and implemenation needs to occur today?

____

____

Meditation

Dawnos _Oriented_ Album // Track 5 - Clouds

Affirmation

Morning Affirmation _______________________________   Evening Affirmation _______________________________

Pausing   (Write out the times // set alarms)

Morning _____________   Midday _____________   Afternoon _____________   Evening _____________

Physical Movement

Walking, Yoga, Running, Weight lifting, Stretching, Jiu Jitsu, Pilates, or another: _______________

Resistance (Tasks for the Day)

Creative ____

Professional ____

Relationship(s) ____

Self ____

Evening Review

How did it go? What lesson(s) did I learn? Who do I need to make an amends with or forgive?

____

____

____

Reading

Turning your thoughts is where freedom begins. When you forgive and let go of negative thoughts about yourself and others, you are freed. This is what repentance actually means. Over time, repentance has been distorted into a word of condemnation, shame, and even violence toward oneself and others. But its deeper meaning is far more humane and hopeful: **a change of mind that leads to a change of direction. In other words—change your thinking.**

We don't change because we are bad. We change because we are good. This is our essence. As we reconnect with Source, we discover that we truly do have the capacity to turn our minds. I see this regularly in my therapeutic work. When someone is in grief, despair, or depression, it often reflects—consciously or unconsciously—a turning toward a negative belief, a false reality that has come to feel absolute. Our thinking has the power to shape our inner state.

I know this can sound Pollyannaish; it once did to me. But notice what happens when you anchor yourself to a single affirmation in the morning and return to it again and again. That thought becomes a tether. It holds you steady, even as the ego mind—the mind of fear—spins a convincing and relentless story. So today, allow yourself to turn. Anchor into the thought you wish were true, the one you almost don't trust yet. Remember it throughout the day. As a mentor once told me, *if it feels too good to be true, then it must be true.*

Journaling

What am I believing and experiencing today (emotionally, physically and spiritually)? What is my positive mindset and my negative mindset? How can I reparent myself with my current situation? What would the voice of Love say?

____

____

____

____

____

____

____

Vision

Reconnect to your Vision // What structure and implemenation needs to occur today?

____

____

Meditation

Dawnos *Disoriented* Album // Track 2 - Voice of Love

Affirmation

Morning Affirmation _____________________________   Evening Affirmation _____________________________

Pausing   (Write out the times // set alarms)

Morning ____________   Midday ____________   Afternoon ____________   Evening ____________

Physical Movement

Walking, Yoga, Running, Weight lifting, Stretching, Jiu Jitsu, Pilates, or another: ______________

Resistance (Tasks for the Day)

Creative ____

Professional ____

Relationship(s) ____

Self ____

Evening Review

How did it go? What lesson(s) did I learn? Who do I need to make an amends with or forgive?

____

____

____

Mod 5 // Day 7

Reading

With all the negativity not only in the world—just read the news—but also within us, there is a kind of detox that needs to occur. Much of the time we live with an undercurrent of rumination, resentment, or anxious thoughts running quietly in the background. When we begin to step out of that pattern, it's very normal to feel discomfort, even a temporary increase in emotional dysregulation. If we've been ignoring ourselves, staying busy, or subtly running, slowing down and turning inward can feel unsettling at first. **The good news is that this phase is temporary.**

Think of it like hill sprints. You push your body to its edge, your heart rate spikes, and everything feels intense—yet you trust that your body knows how to regulate again. Or imagine stepping into a cold plunge. The first moments are shocking, almost overwhelming, but if you stay present, the body adapts. What both experiences require is a focus point—something steady to place your attention on.

In those moments, focusing on a single point can be remarkably effective. In therapy, this is similar to brainspotting: you gently fix your attention on one spot in your field of vision that holds a sense of strength or stability, while allowing awareness of the periphery to remain. You stay with that focus for as long as needed—minutes, sometimes longer. It's a kind of hyper-focused mindfulness. **As attention settles, thinking naturally slows, and in some moments the mind becomes completely quiet. In essence, you enter a state of flow while simultaneously enduring an intense physiological or emotional experience—and something inside begins to recalibrate.**

Journaling

What am I believing and experiencing today (emotionally, physically and spiritually)? What is my positive mindset and my negative mindset? How can I reparent myself with my current situation? What would the voice of Love say?

Vision

Reconnect to your Vision // What structure and implemenation needs to occur today?

____

____

Meditation

Dawnos Disoriented Album // Track 3 - Focus Point

Affirmation

Morning Affirmation _______________________________   Evening Affirmation _______________________________

Pausing   (Write out the times // set alarms)

Morning ______________   Midday ______________   Afternoon ______________   Evening ______________

Physical Movement

Walking, Yoga, Running, Weight lifting, Stretching, Jiu Jitsu, Pilates, or another: ______________

Resistance (Tasks for the Day)

Creative ____

Professional ____

Relationship(s) ____

Self ____

Evening Review

How did it go? What lesson(s) did I learn? Who do I need to make an amends with or forgive?

____

____

Six

Emotions

I remember the very first time I was in therapy and really got serious about it, nearly 20 years ago. The therapist at the time had a list of emotions on the floor: glad, sad, fear, anger, hurt, lonely, shame, and guilt. As I read those, I asked why there was one positive emotion and all the rest negative. I grew up in a family where we did the emotion of "glad" really well. But we didn't know how to name or identify the other emotions. So that particular stage of my life, I learned to name what I was feeling. That was a very helpful process for me—to name and know what I was feeling. Because these emotions are a part of me, and they're a beautiful symphony in the dance of being human. Here's the problem, though. And this is still prevalent in the therapeutic world and culture today: when we identify by saying "I'm sad," we give too much power to the emotion. It's healthier to say, "I notice a feeling of sadness." Because then the emotion has its place, but at the moment we say "I am," we're over-identifying with the emotion. We're saying that is who we are. This might feel like a subtle technicality, a nuanced distinction. But it's bigger than that. The work is, yes, to identify the emotion. To allow it to be the energy it is. It's a signal. It's telling you something. **Remember this: We cannot control the emotion that comes into our awareness.** When the emotion comes in, it's coming in. It's showing up for a reason. It's a messenger. It's a signal. It's a guest—though often an uninvited guest. But if we over-identify with it, similar to the body, we begin to serve the emotion instead of having mastery over it.

So instead of serving the emotion—which often happens when we're drowning in it, or on the flip side, over-identifying by saying "I am this emotion"—the healthier practice is: "Oh, I notice this. What is this telling me? What's the signal here?" Caution: We tend to project the emotion, assigning it to the situation around us. But the more evolved move is to go inward and ask, "What's happening inside of me? Why is this showing up for me?" It's a beautiful sign to inquire and go inward. It's data calling you to go inward, to ask what's going on inside—all for the purpose of integrating even more. Emotions aren't the enemy. They're not something to suppress or avoid. But they're also not who you are. **They're information. They're messengers. They're part of the human experience, but they don't define you. When you can hold this distinction—when you can notice emotions without becoming them—you develop emotional mastery.** Not control. Not suppression. But the ability to be with your emotions without being consumed by them. This is the work. Not to eliminate emotions, but to relate to them differently. To honor them as signals while maintaining your position as the observer, the one who notices, the one who remains whole even as feelings come and go. So in this module, we'll explore how to work with emotions in this way—honoring them, listening to them, learning from them, without losing yourself in them. This is how we grow. This is how we integrate. This is how we become whole.

Mod 6 // Day 1

Reading

There are mornings when life feels like Groundhog Day. You wake up and it's just another day—going through the motions, searching for some spark of joy or purpose, feeling vaguely off without knowing why. Maybe you feel anxious and frustrated. Maybe there's a quiet guilt whispering that you're not enough. Maybe you're just sad for no apparent reason you can name. These are the mornings when sitting with yourself matters most. This is what you owe yourself: to sit long enough that the wound can appear. Not to bring more pain, but to bring healing. Not to punish you, but to free you. When you give yourself this time, something remarkable happens. You can finally meet what's hurting in a new way—a healing way.

Here's the truth about our ego: it's nothing more than a collection of lost inner child parts. Fragments of us that got scared, rejected, or hurt along the way. They've been running the show from the shadows, trying to protect us through anxiety, guilt, and self-criticism. These parts don't need to be fought or fixed. They need to be brought in, nurtured, sat with, explored. They need to become one with you again. When you face the emotions, behaviors, or past actions that have brought guilt and pain—when you invite them in by truly feeling them and seeing them through the mind of Love—something shifts. Peace comes. Release happens. Wholeness begins to emerge. This is the healing work. Not analyzing or explaining your feelings away, but being with them. Seeing them through eyes of compassion rather than judgment. So today, whatever rises in you—the frustration, the sadness, the guilt, the sense that something is off—invite it in. Don't push it away. Don't try to fix it or understand it or make it go away. Just be with it. See it through the eyes of love. That lost part of you has been waiting a long time to be welcomed home. This is how we become whole. This is how we heal. This is how we finally break free from Groundhog Day. Sit with yourself. The wound will appear. And when it does, meet it with love.

Journaling

What am I believing and experiencing today (emotionally, physically and spiritually)? What is my positive mindset and my negative mindset? How can I reparent myself with my current situation? What would the voice of Love say?

____

____

____

____

____

____

Vision

Reconnect to your Vision // What structure and implemenation needs to occur today?

____

____

Meditation

Dawnos _Disoriented_ Album // Track 4 – Emotional Cycle

Affirmation

Morning Affirmation _______________________________   Evening Affirmation _______________________________

Pausing **(Write out the times // set alarms)**

Morning _____________   Midday _____________   Afternoon _____________   Evening _____________

Physical Movement

Walking, Yoga, Running, Weight lifting, Stretching, Jiu Jitsu, Pilates, or another: _______________

Resistance (Tasks for the Day)

Creative ____

Professional ____

Relationship(s) ____

Self ____

Evening Review

How did it go? What lesson(s) did I learn? Who do I need to make an amends with or forgive?

____

____

Mod 6 // Day 2

Reading

Emotional mastery—the practice of envisioning your life situations or inner state as already fully realized—is not wishful fantasy, as I once believed. It's a discipline rooted in how humans actually learn and adapt. Great athletes do this instinctively. They visualize running their plays, rehearsing outcomes with the end already in mind. Successful business leaders do the same—envisioning a company that is already functioning, aligned, and fulfilled long before it fully exists.

This practice applies just as powerfully to our inner lives and relationships. Whether the vision involves an external accomplishment or an interpersonal way of being, emotional mastery becomes a formative tool. Often in the morning, I envision myself as my most evolved self—especially in how I want to show up with my wife and children, particularly when we may be struggling or not at our best. I'll even imagine a familiar moment of tension: one of us frustrated, the beginning of a negative cycle that I know well. Then comes the shift in practice. Instead of rehearsing the old pattern, I allow myself to see and feel myself meeting that moment from my most grounded, integrated place. I stay with it—meditating on what my body would feel like, the emotional tone, the posture, the words I would choose, the actions I would take. And then I allow myself to enjoy it.

In doing this, I'm not bypassing reality—I'm training my nervous system and attention to recognize a truer option. I'm living from the end and gently bringing that state into the present moment. When I do, something changes naturally. My responses soften. My awareness widens. And the way I live that day begins to align, not through effort, but through embodiment.

Journaling

What am I believing and experiencing today (emotionally, physically and spiritually)? What is my positive mindset and my negative mindset? How can I reparent myself with my current situation? What would the voice of Love say?

____

____

____

____

____

____

____

Vision

Reconnect to your Vision // What structure and implemenation needs to occur today?

____

____

Meditation

Dawnos *Disoriented* Album // Track 5 – Emotional Mastery

Affirmation

Morning Affirmation _______________________   Evening Affirmation _______________________

Pausing   (Write out the times // set alarms)

Morning ______________   Midday ______________   Afternoon ______________   Evening ______________

Physical Movement

Walking, Yoga, Running, Weight lifting, Stretching, Jiu Jitsu, Pilates, or another: ______________

Resistance (Tasks for the Day)

Creative ____

Professional ____

Relationship(s) ____

Self ____

Evening Review

How did it go? What lesson(s) did I learn? Who do I need to make an amends with or forgive?

____

____

Mod 6 // Day 3

Reading

What we once thought of as conquering the dragon is, as Joseph Campbell suggests, the act of facing the dragon—and in doing so, facing and transforming ourselves. This is not accomplished through defeat or the killing of the metaphorical dragon, as that belongs to an old dualistic way of thinking. The true work is integration: bringing back that which was lost. The impulse to push away or defeat the "bad" or "evil" parts of ourselves only perpetuates the vicious cycle. When these parts are met with judgment or rejection, they do not dissolve; they harden. But when we learn to look at them with compassion, through a new lens of love, something begins to shift. This does not mean we condone harmful behavior. Rather, we learn to love the place from which the behavior arises—which is always a wounded place. This is how peace is made with oneself.

The great task each of us faces is the courage to be uncomfortable—to sit with whatever emotion is present and allow it to transform. Grief, when allowed to fully move through us, deepens our capacity. Anger brings courage and resolve. Fear brings awakening and alertness. Over time, we learn to grow in our ability to hold all of it. In this way, we are no longer against ourselves or against others. We begin to see that all of it—and yes, all of it—is a gift. When we stop chasing only pleasure or bliss, we learn to be present with whatever arises, trusting that each experience has something to offer. And because we now have tools—breath, integration, emotional mastery, and connection to the inner loving parent—the inner child is no longer alone or abandoned. We become the ones who provide the safety, the steadiness, and the peace within.

Journaling

What am I believing and experiencing today (emotionally, physically and spiritually)? What is my positive mindset and my negative mindset? How can I reparent myself with my current situation? What would the voice of Love say?

____

____

____

____

____

____

____

____

Vision

Reconnect to your Vision // What structure and implemenation needs to occur today?

____

____

Meditation

Dawnos _Disoriented_ Album // Track 6 – Capacity

Affirmation

Morning Affirmation ______________________________   Evening Affirmation __________________________________

Pausing (Write out the times // set alarms)

Morning ______________   Midday ______________   Afternoon ______________   Evening ______________

Physical Movement

Walking, Yoga, Running, Weight lifting, Stretching, Jiu Jitsu, Pilates, or another: ________________

Resistance (Tasks for the Day)

Creative ____

Professional ____

Relationship(s) ____

Self ____

Evening Review

How did it go? What lesson(s) did I learn? Who do I need to make an amends with or forgive?

____

____

Mod 6 // Day 4

Reading

As I wake up, I notice a familiar undercurrent—negative energy, fear, resentment, and, more than anything, old grievances toward myself. Beneath it all is a deep, ancient feeling: I am not enough. But when I slow down and really see this part of me, something softens. I can feel compassion. I can even smile. This is my second-grade self—the boy who first learned to doubt himself. So much of who I am today, both the struggle and the strength, grew from this place. It is this same part of me that wakes me up at 4:45 each morning, driven to fulfill a vision I have carried for years. If it weren't for the difficulty I had with school, with reading, with dyslexia, I don't know if that drive would exist in quite the same way. This place holds both determination and insecurity. It still longs for reassurance—that the vision will work, that the path is true.

There have been times when the path felt wild, even reckless—100% commission in commercial real estate, graduate school twice, deeper callings that demanded trust and surrender. And yet, when I look back, it has always worked out. More than that, each time I followed the deeper pull within me, it led to expansion. **Through all these various life pivots I've learned this: when I go with the flow—when I trust what my deeper self is calling me toward—life carries me.** When I hesitate, when I cling to control, I struggle. It's like standing in a flowing stream. The moment I grab the edge, the water presses against me. When I let go, it moves with me. So today, I invite you to do the same. Return to the most painful place within you. Meet it with compassion. Offer encouragement. Trust this truth: not only will it work out, it will fully expand you if you give yourself over to the process. Now, access your deepest and highest self. Imagine yourself at eighty years old. What would your eighty-year-old self say to you today? Write it down. Let this become your affirmation.

Journaling

What am I believing and experiencing today (emotionally, physically and spiritually)? What is my positive mindset and my negative mindset? How can I reparent myself with my current situation? What would the voice of Love say?

____

____

____

____

____

____

Vision

Reconnect to your Vision // What structure and implemenation needs to occur today?

____

____

Meditation

Dawnos _Air_ Album // Track 4 – Expansion

Affirmation

Morning Affirmation ______________________________   Evening Affirmation ______________________________

Pausing   (Write out the times // set alarms)

Morning _____________   Midday _____________   Afternoon _____________   Evening _____________

Physical Movement

Walking, Yoga, Running, Weight lifting, Stretching, Jiu Jitsu, Pilates, or another: _______________

Resistance (Tasks for the Day)

Creative ____

Professional ____

Relationship(s) ____

Self ____

Evening Review

How did it go? What lesson(s) did I learn? Who do I need to make an amends with or forgive?

____

____

____

Reading

Spend some time this morning noticing if there is anything in your life you need to let go of. Maybe it's a financial situation, a relationship, an old pattern, or a harmful habit. Maybe it's the situation you find yourself in right now. Simply bring it to mind. As you do, notice and allow whatever emotions, thoughts, or body sensations arise. You don't need to fix, change, or analyze anything. Just be with what's here. Stay open. Notice the uncertainty in all of it—the unknown aspect—and see if you can allow that to be present without resistance.

Now here's the key. Instead of imagining more negativity—punishment, consequences, fear, or failure—allow yourself to imagine a positive outcome. Let yourself feel what it might be like to experience a sense of wholeness, a sense of inner capacity, or inner stability. Pause for a few moments and allow yourself this gift. Notice what it feels like to be at peace with yourself. Notice how the energy begins to shift. Notice being at peace with others around you. Notice a sense of connection—of being aligned to what is, rather than at odds with it. See that you are no longer fighting against anything. Instead, you are open—to possibility, to growth, to positive outcomes. This isn't about forcing optimism or escaping reality. It's about allowing goodness to be part of what's possible.

Now gently return to where you started—to what you feel called to surrender. Notice, with compassion, the growing ability to let go. And allow yourself to let go and let love—to let love (Source) guide you, hold you, and show you what's next.

Journaling

What am I believing and experiencing today (emotionally, physically and spiritually)? What is my positive mindset and my negative mindset? How can I reparent myself with my current situation? What would the voice of Love say?

____

____

____

____

____

____

____

Vision

Reconnect to your Vision // What structure and implemenation needs to occur today?

____

____

Meditation

Dawnos *Disoriented* Album // Track 5 – Emotional Mastery

Affirmation

Morning Affirmation _____________________________   Evening Affirmation _____________________________

Pausing   (Write out the times // set alarms)

Morning ______________   Midday ______________   Afternoon ______________   Evening ______________

Physical Movement

Walking, Yoga, Running, Weight lifting, Stretching, Jiu Jitsu, Pilates, or another: ________________

Resistance (Tasks for the Day)

Creative ____

Professional ____

Relationship(s) ____

Self ____

Evening Review

How did it go? What lesson(s) did I learn? Who do I need to make an amends with or forgive?

____

____

Mod 6 // Day 6

Reading

When life is busy and the demands are pulling you in various directions, it's all the more important to slow down. There's a saying in Al-Anon: **"Where there is urgency, there is disease." The dis'ease' is of the mind of fear.** Typically, when we're in this state, the idea of stopping even for five minutes makes no sense. We're in busy mode. We think we have to keep going because there's so much to do. The paradox is this: when we slow down, pause, breathe, and remind ourselves of the phrase "easy does it," we're able to get back into alignment. We calm down and remember what and who is important, and the purpose of the day. Maybe it's to be in service to our spouse and kids. Maybe we realign with our affirmation of the day, whatever it may be. The importance of having a clear set of intentions for the day helps provide not only direction but guardrails. It cautions us not to self-sabotage and to keep the main thing the main thing which is love and service to others. When urgency drives you, you're running on fear. When intention guides you, you're moving with love.

The busier you feel, the more you need to pause. The more urgent everything seems, the more you need to slow down. The more scattered your attention becomes, the more you need to return to what matters. Five minutes of stillness can save you hours of frantic, unfocused activity. One deep breath can bring you back from the edge of overwhelm. One moment of remembering your intention can redirect your entire day. So today, when you feel the pull of urgency—when everything feels critical and you can't possibly stop—that's exactly when you need to pause. Breathe. Remember. Realign. Easy does it. Keep the main things the main things: love and service. Everything else can wait. This is not wasted time. This is the most important work you'll do all day.

Journaling

What am I believing and experiencing today (emotionally, physically and spiritually)? What is my positive mindset and my negative mindset? How can I reparent myself with my current situation? What would the voice of Love say?

Vision

Reconnect to your Vision // What structure and implemenation needs to occur today?

____

____

Meditation

Dawnos *Air* Album // Track 2 – Downshift

Affirmation

Morning Affirmation _______________________   Evening Affirmation _______________________

Pausing   (Write out the times // set alarms)

Morning _____________   Midday _____________   Afternoon _____________   Evening _____________

Physical Movement

Walking, Yoga, Running, Weight lifting, Stretching, Jiu Jitsu, Pilates, or another: _______________

Resistance (Tasks for the Day)

Creative ____

Professional ____

Relationship(s) ____

Self ____

Evening Review

How did it go? What lesson(s) did I learn? Who do I need to make an amends with or forgive?

____

____

____

Reading

There may be mornings when you wake up and reflect on the night before, realizing you fell back into old patterns. Maybe it was patterns of judgment or gossip. Perhaps you were emotionally reactive in ways you thought you'd moved beyond. Or it could have been old behaviors that haven't served you well—behaviors that bring back a lot of pain and make you feel like you haven't grown at all. Whatever it may be, it's important to know this: **Being hard on yourself and carrying guilt will not bring healing. The ego has a way of disguising itself in the form of self-improvement that is really fueled by guilt and shame.** This is the classic cycle of addiction: Saying, "I won't do this behavior again." Then fixating and trying not to do it. Then falling back into it. Then feeling guilt and shame afterward. Then vowing not to do it again. And the cycle continues. You are unknowingly being ego-led the entire time—through control, through force, through shame. **The only way out of this cycle is a radical nurture and acceptance of yourself.** To truly allow love in—not just to know it intellectually, but to feel it at your core. When you are willing to accept this forgiveness, you're able to be back in the present moment. And this present moment is love. You are fully loved right now, not after you fix yourself.

Here's a helpful meditative practice: Go back to the moment of error in your mind. But this time, see yourself living it out from your most evolved and higher self. See yourself responding differently—with peace, with clarity, with love. This is not only a way to change your neural pathways. More importantly, it allows you to come back "online" to who you already are. You are not broken. You are not failing. You are human. The pattern will change not through shame and guilt, but through acceptance. Not through control, but through compassion. So this morning, if you're carrying any regret—pause. Breathe. Allow yourself to be forgiven. See yourself as already whole. This is how we heal, how we grow, how we finally break free.

Journaling

What am I believing and experiencing today (emotionally, physically and spiritually)? What is my positive mindset and my negative mindset? How can I reparent myself with my current situation? What would the voice of Love say?

____

____

____

____

____

____

Vision

Reconnect to your Vision // What structure and implemenation needs to occur today?

____

____

Meditation

Dawnos _Oriented_ Album // Track 6 – Sacred Space

Affirmation

Morning Affirmation _______________________________   Evening Affirmation _______________________________

Pausing   (Write out the times // set alarms)

Morning _____________   Midday _____________   Afternoon _____________   Evening _____________

Physical Movement

Walking, Yoga, Running, Weight lifting, Stretching, Jiu Jitsu, Pilates, or another: _______________

Resistance (Tasks for the Day)

Creative ____

Professional ____

Relationship(s) ____

Self ____

Evening Review

How did it go? What lesson(s) did I learn? Who do I need to make an amends with or forgive?

____

____

Notes:

Seven

Smaller Self

As we enter this module on the smaller self, it's important to begin with integration rather than fragmentation. The smaller self—our ego, our separate sense of self—is not something to be rejected or overcome. It is simply a part of us, a confused part, that learned to operate as if it were separate—from our soul, from others, from life itself. This smaller, separate self is not a mistake. It is part of being human, and it plays an essential role in every person's journey. In many ways, it becomes the antagonist in our personal story. And like any true antagonist, it is not inherently good or bad—it is simply the opposing force to the larger self. Even the phrase "smaller self" can be a misnomer, carrying the sense that this part is less evolved or something to be ashamed of. But that's not the case at all. The smaller self is integral. Another way to understand it is as the inner child—an aspect of us that is incredibly necessary and cannot be bypassed.

The smaller self is made up of the parts of us that have been lost. And this is why this state holds both the wound and the gold. Robert Bly writes in *Iron John* that "where we've been wounded is where our genius lies—that's precisely the place from which we'll give our major gift to the community." This golden place becomes an entrance back into innocence and childlike wonder, as well as the parts of us that were disavowed, hidden, or left behind. As we reconnect with the inner child here, something else awakens alongside it: the inner loving parent. Both are needed. As Byron Katie reminds us, "The ego is not an enemy. I literally loved it to death. Be kind. Consider the terror of falseness. The ego is a confused child." Healing, then, is not about eliminating this part, but about learning how to live within the tension of opposites—light and shadow, innocence and wound—holding them together rather than choosing between them.

I've often wondered if this is one way to understand the image of the lost sheep. What if the lost sheep represents one of these lost parts of us? The work is not judgment or correction, but retrieval—going back with love to find what was cut off and bring it home. These are the parts that learned to hide because they didn't feel safe, or shut down because they didn't feel seen. And yet, these very parts hold your genius. They hold your gift. They are where healing happens—not only for you, but for everyone you will touch with your story, your wisdom, and your presence. The work of this module is not only about identification, but about unification. Not rejecting the smaller self, but reclaiming it. Not bypassing the inner child, but becoming the loving parent that child always needed. This is where transformation happens. **This is where wholeness begins. And this wholeness does not arrive all at once. It is built slowly, through relationship—through learning how to stay present with these parts rather than abandoning them again.** In this module, we are not trying to fix the smaller self, manage it, or make it disappear. We are learning how to listen, how to attune, and how to respond from love instead of fear. **This is the movement from fragmentation toward integration, from survival toward trust.** As these inner relationships heal, something quietly reorganizes within us. We become more grounded, more spacious, more whole. And from this place, we begin to live—not from a divided self—but from an integrated one.

Reading

There's something within us that has been present since the beginning—long before we had language for it. This presence is the Inner Child. This isn't just an idea of the inner child—it's a deeply embedded truth within us, held in the unconscious, carried as energy. The inner child can mean a couple of things. **There is the innocent child—the playful one, full of imagination.** This is the part of us from early life when everything was new, when time didn't matter, when we lived in complete presence and total play. We weren't yet aware of ego. We were simply ourselves—at peace—before the world began telling us who we were supposed to be, or who we were not. And then **there is the wounded child. This is the part of us that begins to experience pain**—through school, family systems, expectations, and the particular struggles that were uniquely ours. These are the experiences we learned to carry, and many of them still live within us today.

The practice, then, is to reconnect with these lost parts of ourselves—to the wounded child—and also to the innocent one. Not just to acknowledge them, but to allow them to speak. What's been so powerful for me—and what marked a major shift in my own life—is that through journaling, as I allowed that pure, innocent child to begin speaking, it often sounded like the same voice I've come to know as the voice of Love. A divine inner wisdom. A quiet guidance that doesn't lead us astray. It speaks with childlike faith and childlike wonder.

The beauty is that we are all of it—the innocent child, the wounded child, the whole story. And when we integrate these parts, we bring the fullness of who we are into the world. That integration is what allows our unique imprint—our particular expression of life—to emerge.

Journaling

What am I believing and experiencing today (emotionally, physically and spiritually)? What is my positive mindset and my negative mindset? How can I reparent myself with my current situation? What would the voice of Love say?

____

____

____

____

____

____

____

Vision

Reconnect to your Vision // What structure and implemenation needs to occur today?

____

____

Meditation

Dawnos _Disoriented_ Album // Track 7 – Inner Child

Affirmation

Morning Affirmation ______________________________   Evening Affirmation ______________________________

Pausing   (Write out the times // set alarms)

Morning _____________   Midday _____________   Afternoon _____________   Evening _____________

Physical Movement

Walking, Yoga, Running, Weight lifting, Stretching, Jiu Jitsu, Pilates, or another: _______________

Resistance (Tasks for the Day)

Creative ____

Professional ____

Relationship(s) ____

Self ____

Evening Review

How did it go? What lesson(s) did I learn? Who do I need to make an amends with or forgive?

____

____

Reading

This morning during my daily check-in, I wrote four words that surprised me: *I love my life.* And that has not always been the case. There is so much to be grateful for. And yet, there are also vulnerabilities I'm still navigating, struggles I haven't fully resolved. **Profound gratitude and ongoing insecurity can coexist.** As I sat with this paradox, seeking clarity on areas where I still feel uncertain, something shifted. I had the thought to go back to my younger self. If I could, I'd go back to my high school self—the one playing tennis, feeling less-than because it wasn't football or basketball. I would tell him: *You be you. Play tennis. Who cares about others' opinions? None of this will matter years from now. Have fun with it.* I'd find the kid who wanted a girlfriend so desperately and say: *Enjoy your time with your friends. That amazing woman will find you. You don't have to worry about it.* And to the one struggling with school and dyslexia: *Do your best. The unfolding will happen—college, a degree, all of it. Just enjoy the journey.* As I write this, I realize I need encouragement too. I'm waiting for clarity, for the voice that tells me what's next. And then it comes: *Finish what you've started. You've had a vision—The Holland Method, the curriculum, the book, the workbook. Keep the faith that you are meant to fulfill it.* The truth is, I've loved this process—the daily flow of creating something out of nothing. I sense that what I've learned is meant to be shared, to help bring forth your own unique light.

So here's the practice: Go back to a time when you were hurting or insecure. See your higher self—the current you or the older, wiser you—speaking to that younger version. What wisdom does that younger you need to hear? What reassurance? What permission? Then visualize it. **Imagine yourself living out those younger years differently.** For me, it's this: *Walk through the halls of your high school at peace, confident, with nothing to prove other than you being you.* That is the integration. That is the healing. When we give our younger selves what they needed—even if only in our imagination, even if only now—something shifts. The insecurity loosens its grip. The struggle finds resolution. Your higher self has always been there, waiting to speak to the part of you that needed to hear it. Listen today. Go back. Offer that younger version of yourself the love and wisdom they were searching for. This is how we become whole.

Journaling

What am I believing and experiencing today (emotionally, physically and spiritually)? What is my positive mindset and my negative mindset? How can I reparent myself with my current situation? What would the voice of Love say?

____

____

____

____

____

Vision

Reconnect to your Vision // What structure and implemenation needs to occur today?

____

____

Meditation

Dawnos *Disoriented* Album // Track 8 – Nurturing Figure

Affirmation

Morning Affirmation _________________________________   Evening Affirmation ____________________________________

Pausing   (Write out the times // set alarms)

Morning _____________   Midday _____________   Afternoon _____________   Evening _____________

Physical Movement

Walking, Yoga, Running, Weight lifting, Stretching, Jiu Jitsu, Pilates, or another: _______________

Resistance (Tasks for the Day)

Creative ____

Professional ____

Relationship(s) ____

Self ____

Evening Review

How did it go? What lesson(s) did I learn? Who do I need to make an amends with or forgive?

____

____

Mod 7 // Day 3

Reading

If we are light and love with full access to Source, why do we still struggle? Why do parts of us still feel broken? The truth is, these parts aren't bad—they just need integration. But what does that actually mean and what are we to do, when you're hurting, when you're struggling with what's right in front of you? The tool that is incredibly effective is to reparent yourself. The PARENT tool can be used formally or informally. The formal practice walks you through a series of steps. PARENT is an acronym: **P**art, **A**sk, **R**emember, **E**nvision, **N**urture, **T**ransform.

The informal practice is simpler: identifying the part of you that is hurting or struggling—a part that is either the protector or seemingly feels lost, shut down, cut off, and 'othered'—and you send so much love to it. You talk to it as a loving friend or a family member who needs unconditional love, compassion, and support. Just yesterday, I found myself lost in a story of fear. I was running through future scenarios, which I'm so often prone to do. And rather than telling myself to stop, or distracting myself, or analyzing even more, I've found that when I catch myself 'caught up' in this trance, I talk to him. I love him. As if I was talking to my own child, I tell him it will be okay because I'm with you. That I love him and encourage him. And then something does happen. How can it not, when you give loving energy back to yourself? Think about it. When was the last time you not only told yourself that you loved you, but that you really meant it? This is what it means to reparent yourself. Oddly enough, you are the parent you've been waiting for. You have what that part of you needs. This is how we heal. This is how we become whole.

Journaling

What am I believing and experiencing today (emotionally, physically and spiritually)? What is my positive mindset and my negative mindset? How can I reparent myself with my current situation? What would the voice of Love say?

____

____

____

____

____

____

____

____

Vision

Reconnect to your Vision // What structure and implemenation needs to occur today?

____

____

Meditation

Dawnos _Disoriented_ Album // Track 9 – PARENT

Affirmation

Morning Affirmation _______________________   Evening Affirmation _______________________________

Pausing (Write out the times // set alarms)

Morning _____________   Midday _____________   Afternoon _____________   Evening _____________

Physical Movement

Walking, Yoga, Running, Weight lifting, Stretching, Jiu Jitsu, Pilates, or another: _____________

Resistance (Tasks for the Day)

Creative ____

Professional ____

Relationship(s) ____

Self ____

Evening Review

How did it go? What lesson(s) did I learn? Who do I need to make an amends with or forgive?

____

____

Reading

Take a moment to consider this question: *What would you do if you were fearless?* How would you live your life differently? Is there something you would pursue—or express—that you've held back from because of fear? Now, gently shift your attention to **childlike wonder**. Return to a time in your life when you felt free to play—when curiosity led the way and joy was unforced. Perhaps it was outdoors, in nature, or lost in imagination. Close your eyes for a moment and simply remember. Notice what comes up.

At that time, the inner critic had not yet formed. The ego had not taken shape. This was **original innocence**—a state of being before fear learned how to speak. Now, look at your life again, but this time through the wisdom you carry today. You have lived, learned, and gathered a knowledge that is uniquely yours. No one else holds it in quite the same way. Here is the invitation: **merge these two**. Bring together the childlike wonder and the adult self. The inner child and the inner loving parent. This is integration. When these two aspects of you work together, you are no longer lost in naïve fantasy or weighed down by responsibility. You step onto a conscious, grounded path—a vision only you can see and bring to life. From here, life begins to flow.

Journaling

What am I believing and experiencing today (emotionally, physically and spiritually)? What is my positive mindset and my negative mindset? How can I reparent myself with my current situation? What would the voice of Love say?

____

____

____

____

____

____

____

____

____

____

Vision

Reconnect to your Vision // What structure and implemenation needs to occur today?

____

____

Meditation

Dawnos *Disoriented* Album // Track 7 – Inner Child

Affirmation

Morning Affirmation _______________________   Evening Affirmation _______________________

Pausing   (Write out the times // set alarms)

Morning ____________   Midday ____________   Afternoon ____________   Evening ____________

Physical Movement

Walking, Yoga, Running, Weight lifting, Stretching, Jiu Jitsu, Pilates, or another: ______________

Resistance (Tasks for the Day)

Creative ____

Professional ____

Relationship(s) ____

Self ____

Evening Review

How did it go? What lesson(s) did I learn? Who do I need to make an amends with or forgive?

____

____

Mod 7 // Day 5

Reading

Ever since I was a little boy, there's been one thread in my life that has never left me: running. When I was young, my father would wake me up early in the morning, and we'd head out to the track. I'd run a mile or two while he trained for marathons. During those years, he often repeated a line that stayed with me: *"The race of life is not to the swift, but to those who keep on running."*

Running became a refuge. You can run almost anywhere—no matter where you are, where you're staying, or what season of life you're in. For me, it's always been a way to think, to sort things out, to have space. But more than that, it's been a way to reconnect with something essential. At that early age, *Chariots of Fire* was everywhere—winning Best Picture, that iconic music playing over and over. That theme still moves me everytime I hear it. And I've always loved what Eric Liddell said: *"When I run, I feel God's pleasure."*

That's what this is really about—returning to the essence of who you are. Remembering what was always true. What stirred you early on. What felt uniquely yours before the world layered expectations and noise on top of it. That energy is still alive. It's what carries you. And it's often where you'll feel the presence of God most clearly. My question to you is are you connected back to that childlike place where you feel God pleasure?

Journaling

What am I believing and experiencing today (emotionally, physically and spiritually)? What is my positive mindset and my negative mindset? How can I reparent myself with my current situation? What would the voice of Love say?

____

____

____

____

____

____

____

____

Vision

Reconnect to your Vision // What structure and implemenation needs to occur today?

____

____

Meditation

Dawnos *Air* Album // Track 6 – Rhythm

Affirmation

Morning Affirmation ___________________________________ Evening Affirmation _____________________________________

Pausing (Write out the times // set alarms)

Morning _____________ Midday _____________ Afternoon _____________ Evening _____________

Physical Movement

Walking, Yoga, Running, Weight lifting, Stretching, Jiu Jitsu, Pilates, or another: ________________

Resistance (Tasks for the Day)

Creative ____

Professional ____

Relationship(s) ____

Self ____

Evening Review

How did it go? What lesson(s) did I learn? Who do I need to make an amends with or forgive?

____

____

Reading

There are moments when our angry adolescent just shows up. When that happens, there are three simple movements to work with it. First, address it. Look at it. Tell the truth about what's there. Second, engage the part that's feeling frustrated—or, more honestly, tired or afraid. And third, re-inherit it. Let it go. Make whatever amends or adjustments to yourself or others that you need to make, and then move on.

I had a moment like this recently on a ski trip. It was almost comical—the kid in me got frustrated: lugging my skis, feeling tired and overheated, realizing I couldn't find my lift ticket, then having to walk all the way back to the car. I could feel the irritation building. I tried to hold it in—and if you've ever done that, you know how that usually goes. Of course, after the whole ordeal, I found the lift ticket in my jacket. It wasn't the version of myself I wanted to be showing up as. But it was a part of me nonetheless.

And that's the work—to own what needs to be owned. To **take 100% responsibility without turning that responsibility into self-punishment.** To not treat ourselves harshly. We learn from it, we try to do it differently next time, and then we move on. We let ourselves enjoy the day that's still in front of us. **Every now and then, our shadow still comes out. That's just reality.** Mine can be frustrating and a little bratty at times. It's there. It's part of my humanity. But the more we can own it, move on, and bring compassion back to ourselves, the more freedom we have. Sometimes things are just frustrating—not because we're failing, but because we're human.

Journaling

What am I believing and experiencing today (emotionally, physically and spiritually)? What is my positive mindset and my negative mindset? How can I reparent myself with my current situation? What would the voice of Love say?

____

____

____

____

____

____

____

____

Vision

Reconnect to your Vision // What structure and implemenation needs to occur today?

____

____

Meditation

Dawnos *Disoriented* Album // Track 8 – Nurturing Figure

Affirmation

Morning Affirmation ___________________________   Evening Affirmation _______________________________

Pausing   (Write out the times // set alarms)

Morning ____________   Midday ____________   Afternoon ____________   Evening ____________

Physical Movement

Walking, Yoga, Running, Weight lifting, Stretching, Jiu Jitsu, Pilates, or another: ______________

Resistance (Tasks for the Day)

Creative ____

Professional ____

Relationship(s) ____

Self ____

Evening Review

How did it go? What lesson(s) did I learn? Who do I need to make an amends with or forgive?

____

____

Mod 7 // Day 7

Reading

Lately, I've made a decision to eliminate certain foods, especially sugar. I've found that I feel better and eat less. It required making a firm choice, and it had been going really well—I've been feeling great. Until yesterday. Yesterday was Thanksgiving, and when I saw a certain piece of pie, I caved. On one hand, of course, this is Thanksgiving—why not just enjoy it and loosen up? On the other hand, I had told myself, and even mentioned to a friend in a joking, laughing way, that I wasn't going to eat sweets. Well, I chose the former. I had a piece of pie, which turned into two. And then cookies later on. By that evening, I felt physically sick—mostly from all the food I ate. I just wasn't feeling good.

I know this may seem like a mild story when it comes to falling back into old patterns. I even have a voice that says it's not a big deal. But the point I want to make is this: I've found an ideal way that I want to live my life. It's like my higher self is showing me a path. When I don't fully abide by it and fall back into less ideal patterns, the lesson I've learned is to be gentle on myself—not hard. There have been other patterns in my life that have been harder to break and have carried heavier effects. **The truth is, there's a cause and effect to every decision we make. But the beauty—the miracle—lies in gently reparenting yourself.** You can tell yourself, "Hey, this was just a moment. Let's move on to the next." Get back on the path. Reconnect to the voice within. This voice really does guide us through the unique curriculum that is presented to us each day in this school of life. I'm learning more and more not to take things too seriously, but also to hold myself to a standard that's connected to the vision and ideal way I want to live. Each of us can live our lives fully in a way that is unique to us.

Journaling

What am I believing and experiencing today (emotionally, physically and spiritually)? What is my positive mindset and my negative mindset? How can I reparent myself with my current situation? What would the voice of Love say?

____

____

____

____

____

____

____

Vision

Reconnect to your Vision // What structure and implemenation needs to occur today?

____

____

Meditation

Dawnos _Disoriented_ Album // Track 9 – PARENT

Affirmation

Morning Affirmation _______________________________   Evening Affirmation _______________________________

Pausing   (Write out the times // set alarms)

Morning _____________   Midday _____________   Afternoon _____________   Evening _____________

Physical Movement

Walking, Yoga, Running, Weight lifting, Stretching, Jiu Jitsu, Pilates, or another: _______________

Resistance (Tasks for the Day)

Creative ____

Professional ____

Relationship(s) ____

Self ____

Evening Review

How did it go? What lesson(s) did I learn? Who do I need to make an amends with or forgive?

____

____

____

Notes:

Eight

Grief

If there's one phrase to describe grief, it's this: **We grieve when we lose something or someone we loved. And it's been said beautifully that we can choose when to celebrate, but we don't get to choose when to grieve. Grief comes upon us.** It's how we grieve that is paramount. There's also an important distinction to understand: two experiences often weave in and out together—the dark night of the soul and depression. Both will look the same on the surface. To grieve, to truly grieve, is honoring the dark night, which could also be a state of depression. And that's not an indictment on yourself. That is oftentimes part of the territory. The question is: How do we grieve in a way that will lead to heart expansion rather than heart closing? And this is where it's key. Through this state of grief, if there's one thing to pass on, it's this: Do not close your heart off to love. If you do, that's when we become cynical, bitter. We over-identify and we become the victim. Instead, we move into it.

The poet David Whyte defines zen as heartbreak. Think about that. There's something paradoxical about peace, tranquility, and heartbreak existing together. This is the doorway. Grief is an entrance into a deeper state. And if you can have faith and trust that what is occurring right now will pass—that peace will be here—you'll find your way through. There will be a day when, while you'll say you never want to experience this again, you're also thankful. You come to a place of peace. It will no longer hurt as it hurts today because you see what this heartbreak has turned into: a heart opening. Your heart has expanded into a new area of your life you didn't see before. This is the gift hidden inside the grief. Not that the grief itself is good, but that when you don't close your heart to it—when you allow the heartbreak to do its work—it cracks you open in ways that ultimately expand your capacity to love, to feel, to be fully alive. Grief is not the problem. Closing your heart is. So if you're in grief today, you don't have to be "over it" or on anyone else's timeline. But please, whatever you do, don't close your heart. Stay open as you feel it and allow it to move through you. This heartbreak is doing something. It's opening you to a deeper capacity for love, for compassion, for presence. **Trust the heartbreak, even when it hurts, especially when it hurts. The doorway through grief is not around it or over it. It's towards it, with an open heart.** This is how we grieve in a way that leads to expansion. This is how heartbreak becomes heart opening. Stay open. The peace is coming.

Mod 8 // Day 1

Reading

I often sense and feel this dread on Sunday afternoons when traveling and leaving my family. This existential ache—I've had it all my life. It feels like a doorway into this metaphorical cave, this cave I've lived with. Especially several years ago when I went through my own dark night of the soul, it felt like there was a permanent residence. And now it periodically shows up. This ache. And in many ways, it seems like we try to structure our entire lives to avoid this cave, which is synonymous with grief. **This grief is also like a cloud that blocks our ability to see the light within us**. So the darkness that we feel creates all the ingredients for the ego's justification that this nightmare is the lowercase "r" reality. And while grief itself is part of the human experience and signifies that something of importance is now absent, it also doesn't mean that you have to go into this cave and live there, or go into it without a flashlight. This flashlight is your Spirit. Here is the capital "R" Reality: You can bring light into any situation and circumstance. This light comes only from within. Period.

So the practice is to see the grief, see it as a cloud of darkness, and not only engage it but practice meditatively seeing through it with your light. First, with your eyes closed, focus on a light within. Stay in that state until you begin to sense this light and begin to search for it. It's there. Then begin to see the light and allow it to surround you. Then listen for this voice of Love. The ever still, small voice speaking, guiding you within and throughout your life, circumstances, and situations. Here's the truth: You and I are never alone. The darkness wants you to believe you're alone. The light reminds you that you never are.

Journaling

What am I believing and experiencing today (emotionally, physically and spiritually)? What is my positive mindset and my negative mindset? How can I reparent myself with my current situation? What would the voice of Love say?

____

____

____

____

____

____

____

____

Vision

Reconnect to your Vision // What structure and implemenation needs to occur today?

____

____

Meditation

Dawnos _Oriented_ Album // Track 9 – Healing Light

Affirmation

Morning Affirmation _______________________________   Evening Affirmation _______________________________

Pausing   **(Write out the times // set alarms)**

Morning _____________   Midday _____________   Afternoon _______________   Evening _______________

Physical Movement

Walking, Yoga, Running, Weight lifting, Stretching, Jiu Jitsu, Pilates, or another: _______________

Resistance (Tasks for the Day)

Creative ____

Professional ____

Relationship(s) ____

Self ____

Evening Review

How did it go? What lesson(s) did I learn? Who do I need to make an amends with or forgive?

____

____

Reading

There's a classic Jungian concept: the tension of opposites. And the tension of opposites, especially in the grief stage, is both despair and hope. There's a delicate balance here. On one side, there's the danger of spiritual bypass—disavowing the despair, the sorrow and the grief by trying to be overly positive. But then there's another caution: falling too much into despair where you give yourself over to it completely, closing yourself off to hope. This isn't the false type of hope where others try to pull you out of it with platitudes. During one's state of grief, it's about embracing and coming to honor the disappointment, the heartbreak of what was there—whether it's the letting go of a relationship, a marriage, a financial dream, a job, a loved one through death. Because you're human. And who's going to tell you that you can't grieve? It is the loss of that person, that idea, that situation that tells you the meaning. Because we feel the love most poignantly in the beginnings and endings. And so in the midst of this grief, you hold both despair and hope on either side, and here you are in the middle.

I recently heard in a sermon where the rector said: rather than the church giving all the answers, what if we could provide room and space for the mystery and allow for more questions than answers? And here you are in that state of questions. And certainly, there's nothing wrong with that. **In a spiritual sense, you are in the middle of the crucifixion and the resurrection. And there's nowhere to go but just to be within it and to honor your pain because you're human. This is the sacred space of the already and not yet.** You don't have to force positivity. But you also don't have to surrender completely to despair. You hold both. The grief and the possibility. The loss and the mystery. The crucifixion and the faint, distant promise of resurrection. This is where transformation happens. The holy ground is in the middle.

Journaling

What am I believing and experiencing today (emotionally, physically and spiritually)? What is my positive mindset and my negative mindset? How can I reparent myself with my current situation? What would the voice of Love say?

____

____

____

____

____

____

Vision

Reconnect to your Vision // What structure and implemenation needs to occur today?

____

____

Meditation

Dawnos *Disoriented* Album // Track 10 – Parts Integration

Affirmation

Morning Affirmation _______________________   Evening Affirmation _______________________

Pausing   (Write out the times // set alarms)

Morning _____________   Midday _____________   Afternoon _____________   Evening _____________

Physical Movement

Walking, Yoga, Running, Weight lifting, Stretching, Jiu Jitsu, Pilates, or another: _______________

Resistance (Tasks for the Day)

Creative ____

Professional ____

Relationship(s) ____

Self ____

Evening Review

How did it go? What lesson(s) did I learn? Who do I need to make an amends with or forgive?

____

____

____

Mod 8 // Day 3

Reading

There is something about grief and powerlessness that drops you into total confusion. A place where the old maps stop working. You don't know what to do, where to turn, or what step comes next. The nervous system is overwhelmed. The mind reaches for certainty, but none is available. It's here—right in this moment—that the work simplifies. Not because it's easy, but because complexity only adds to the weight. **This is when you return to the most basic elements. You trust the process. You trust the daily practice. You narrow your focus.** Something I've learned from jiu-jitsu is that when you first start, everything feels chaotic. There are positions, transitions, grips, escapes—layers upon layers. Your body doesn't yet know where it is in space. The instinct is to tense, to rush, to force something. But early jiu-jitsu isn't about submissions. It's about principles of keeping your frame intact. You learn to breathe under pressure. You learn posture, base, and frame. You protect your neck. You keep your elbows in. You don't panic. You assess where you are and respond to what's actually happening, and not react out of fear. When things get overwhelming, you return to fundamentals. You slow your breathing. You stay connected to the mat. You hold your frame—not rigid, but responsive. One move at a time.

The same is true in grief and powerlessness. Whether you're deep in loss or stuck in a season that feels inescapable, you don't try to solve your whole life. You don't figure out the future. You come back to the daily rhythm. You hold to one thing. Maybe today that one thing is an affirmation. Maybe it's coming back into your body, to your core. Maybe it's using The Questions that shift you from the mind of fear to the mind of Love. You're not starting from zero—you're remembering what you've already practiced. Strength comes from staying connected to the center. You don't abandon your frame. You don't collapse under pressure. And when confusion clouds your vision and powerlessness presses in, you do the same. You don't give over. You don't abandon yourself. You breathe. You stay with the basics.

Journaling

What am I believing and experiencing today (emotionally, physically and spiritually)? What is my positive mindset and my negative mindset? How can I reparent myself with my current situation? What would the voice of Love say?

Vision

Reconnect to your Vision // What structure and implemenation needs to occur today?

____

____

Meditation

Dawnos *Disoriented* Album // Track 1 – The Questions

Affirmation

Morning Affirmation _______________________   Evening Affirmation _______________________

Pausing (Write out the times // set alarms)

Morning ____________   Midday ____________   Afternoon ____________   Evening ____________

Physical Movement

Walking, Yoga, Running, Weight lifting, Stretching, Jiu Jitsu, Pilates, or another: _______________

Resistance (Tasks for the Day)

Creative ____

Professional ____

Relationship(s) ____

Self ____

Evening Review

How did it go? What lesson(s) did I learn? Who do I need to make an amends with or forgive?

____

____

Mod 8 // Day 4

Reading

One of my favorite movies is Rudy. It's the story of a young man who didn't have the genetic framework or physical build to play football. He was short in stature, but massive in heart. His dream was simple and unwavering: to play football, to run out onto the field at Notre Dame. No one in his family had ever been to college. Nearly everyone doubted the dream. But he never let go of it. There's a poignant stretch in the film where his grieving doesn't look dramatic—it looks devoted. He's attending community college, down to his final semester. If he doesn't get accepted to Notre Dame, the door closes. The dream ends. There's a scene where he's running through the tunnels of the football stadium. At that point, the only way he could stay connected was by working at the stadium. He lived in one of the small rooms in the stadium just to make ends meet. And what you see, day after day, is simple faithfulness: studying and training, studying and training.

Part of grief—and part of this whole process—is devotion. Getting up every morning. Trusting your process. Staying committed to what's true for you. And not giving up on hope, even when all the odds are stacked against you. And when you really give yourself to this devotion, something meets you there. There's a great strength that rises up—quiet, steady, and real. It takes an enormous amount of courage. But if you can almost abandon yourself to the fear and go anyway, I promise you, a strength will meet you on the other side. It's not bravado. It's clarity and passion. It reminds me of that phrase from Friday Night Lights—*clear eyes, full heart, can't lose.* When your eyes are clear and your heart is full, you're no longer fighting yourself. And from that place, no matter the outcome, you haven't lost.

Journaling

What am I believing and experiencing today (emotionally, physically and spiritually)? What is my positive mindset and my negative mindset? How can I reparent myself with my current situation? What would the voice of Love say?

____

____

____

____

____

____

____

Vision

Reconnect to your Vision // What structure and implemenation needs to occur today?

____

____

Meditation

Dawnos _Air_ Album // Track 6 – Rhythm

Affirmation

Morning Affirmation ______________________________   Evening Affirmation __________________________________

Pausing   (Write out the times // set alarms)

Morning _____________   Midday _____________   Afternoon _____________   Evening _____________

Physical Movement

Walking, Yoga, Running, Weight lifting, Stretching, Jiu Jitsu, Pilates, or another: _______________

Resistance (Tasks for the Day)

Creative ____

Professional ____

Relationship(s) ____

Self ____

Evening Review

How did it go? What lesson(s) did I learn? Who do I need to make an amends with or forgive?

____

____

Mod 8 // Day 5

Reading

Dear friend—this journey, this life—wherever you are this morning, I want to invite something in. If there's one word to bring forth, especially for this module on grief, it's **equanimity. It's being at peace with yourself and being at peace with others.** If you truly believe you are connected—as spiritual texts say, a child of God—and really believe it, something begins to shift. What's striking is how easily we forget that this is actually true. That there is a loving, benevolent force, always present, guiding us toward peace and fulfillment. And yet, we slip into forgetfulness instead of forgiveness. We fall into the trance. Sometimes we wake up already off—already carrying the subtle belief that this life is on our shoulders, that it's all up to us to figure it out.

Often, equanimity requires emptying the cup—letting go of what we're holding so it can be filled again in a new way. We loosen our grip on the smaller self so we can move into expansion. This is the flow of life. It's the nature of things. It's the path set before each of us, in our own unique and beautiful curriculum. So today, if you can, center in. Look gently at the thing you're holding. Look at what you're struggling with. Look at the situation—and allow yourself to see it from a different angle. Let love, hope, and promise speak to you. Go radical. Go radical in the amount of love you offer yourself. Do not abandon yourself here. Because when you are at peace with yourself, that peace naturally flows outward to others. This is integration. This is equanimity.

This reflection came to me while I was running along the cliff ridge on Signal Mountain this morning. I am looking out at a beautiful sunrise. It's always faithful. It shows up every day. *My mercies are new every morning; great is Thy faithfulness.* That old hymn was played at my brother's funeral. And here I am—more than twenty-five years later—and it remains just as true. The sun still rises. So enjoy it. And allow yourself to be loved today.

Journaling

What am I believing and experiencing today (emotionally, physically and spiritually)? What is my positive mindset and my negative mindset? How can I reparent myself with my current situation? What would the voice of Love say?

____

____

____

____

____

____

Vision

Reconnect to your Vision // What structure and implemenation needs to occur today?

____

____

Meditation

Dawnos *Disoriented* Album // Track 10 – Parts Integration

Affirmation

Morning Affirmation ______________________________   Evening Affirmation ______________________________

Pausing   (Write out the times // set alarms)

Morning ______________   Midday ______________   Afternoon ______________   Evening ______________

Physical Movement

Walking, Yoga, Running, Weight lifting, Stretching, Jiu Jitsu, Pilates, or another: ______________

Resistance (Tasks for the Day)

Creative ____

Professional ____

Relationship(s) ____

Self ____

Evening Review

How did it go? What lesson(s) did I learn? Who do I need to make an amends with or forgive?

____

____

Mod 8 // Day 6

Reading

What if, after all the work, devotion, struggle, time, and resources, the vision doesn't come to pass? Really sit with this question. And then ask yourself: Whose purpose are you serving this for? **If it's in service to the smaller self—ego promotion, external validation, proof of your worth—then you will see it through the lens of fear and scarcity. And failure will appear real.** But if you see through the eyes of the Larger Self, how can there be failure? There is no failure because you're fulfilling this vision for you and in service to Source. Everything—and I mean everything—depends on how we see it and interpret it. **There is a repeated theme when it comes to creativity: the focus, the guiding light, the "taste," if you will, is to create what you like, not what you think others will like.** The moment you go down that path—creating for what others would like—you have subjugated your vision, your taste, your guiding light to others. And in essence, you are serving the machine. Not Source. Because if you come back to the heart of it all—why you are doing what you're doing, the life you are living, and for what purpose—you realize this: you really only care about, and are doing this for, an audience of One. You with God. God with you. Failure doesn't exist in this relationship. How can it?

When you create from this place, the outcome is not success or failure. The outcome is fulfillment and alignment. The act of showing up and saying "yes" to what you've been called to create. You may not get the recognition you hoped for. The project may not reach as many people as you imagined. The financial return may be less than you needed it to be. But none of that measures what truly matters. It doesn't mean you failed. It means you were faithful. And faithfulness—living from the larger Self, creating in service to Source—is the only success that matters. So if the vision doesn't come to pass in the way you thought it would, ask yourself: Did I show up? Did I do the work? Did I create from love rather than fear? **If the answer is yes, then you succeeded. Because you served the audience of One. And that is all that was ever asked of you.** And here's the mystery: you never know the true impact of what you create because the unfolding is still in process!

Journaling

What am I believing and experiencing today (emotionally, physically and spiritually)? What is my positive mindset and my negative mindset? How can I reparent myself with my current situation? What would the voice of Love say?

____

____

____

____

____

Vision

Reconnect to your Vision // What structure and implemenation needs to occur today?

____

____

Meditation

Dawnos *Oriented* Album // Track 12 – Smile

Affirmation

Morning Affirmation ________________________________   Evening Affirmation ____________________________________

Pausing   (Write out the times // set alarms)

Morning _____________   Midday _____________   Afternoon _____________   Evening _____________

Physical Movement

Walking, Yoga, Running, Weight lifting, Stretching, Jiu Jitsu, Pilates, or another: _______________

Resistance (Tasks for the Day)

Creative ____

Professional ____

Relationship(s) ____

Self ____

Evening Review

How did it go? What lesson(s) did I learn? Who do I need to make an amends with or forgive?

____

____

____

Reading

Grief comes in seasons, and it also comes in moments. There are times when life is generally going well, yet a single situation casts the shadow of an old loss. This is part of the human experience. Grief awakens a sense of separation—it reminds us of what has been lost, what once was, or what we fear may never return. When this shadow appears, the work is not to push through it, but to be gently held within it.

In this practice, we use the Cocoon Meditation in a slightly different way. Rather than placing the focus on you striving to process or fix what you're feeling, you are invited to receive. Begin by visualizing the people who have loved you and encouraged you throughout your life—those who are still here and those who have passed on. See them surrounding you, forming a cocoon of presence and care. One by one, imagine each person offering you exactly what you need in this moment: reassurance, wisdom, strength, tenderness, courage. Allow it to feel as if you are downloading their knowing, their love, their steady confidence in you. As they surround you, let your heart be fueled by **their** compassion and encouragement. Take your time here. Breathe it in slowly. Don't just imagine it—feel it. This feeling matters.

When you allow yourself to emotionally receive, something shifts. The pressure to perform or hold everything together softens. **You move from doing into being, from effort into replenishment.** Stay here as long as you need, breathing in support, breathing out resistance. Let yourself be recharged. Rest and receive today.

Journaling

What am I believing and experiencing today (emotionally, physically and spiritually)? What is my positive mindset and my negative mindset? How can I reparent myself with my current situation? What would the voice of Love say?

Vision

Reconnect to your Vision // What structure and implemenation needs to occur today?

____

____

Meditation

Dawnos _Disoriented_ Album // Track 11 – Cocoon

Affirmation

Morning Affirmation _______________________________   Evening Affirmation _______________________________

Pausing   (Write out the times // set alarms)

Morning _____________   Midday _____________   Afternoon _____________   Evening _____________

Physical Movement

Walking, Yoga, Running, Weight lifting, Stretching, Jiu Jitsu, Pilates, or another: _______________

Resistance (Tasks for the Day)

Creative ____

Professional ____

Relationship(s) ____

Self ____

Evening Review

How did it go? What lesson(s) did I learn? Who do I need to make an amends with or forgive?

____

____

____

Notes:

Powerlessness

The state of powerlessness evokes two different responses from two different minds. From the ego mind, powerlessness triggers fear. The ego knows that a death-like experience is being asked of it, a letting go of control. It casts forth darkness, urgency, and resistance because it senses its own end. But from the mind of Love, powerlessness is realized as salvation. Because this ego mind is the very block and reason we all stay separate and small. Its death is our liberation. When we first enter this state, we experience a metaphorical darkness, but only because we're still seeing through the ego mind. This is actually very good news. It is a good and wise thing to say, "I don't know," because it means we have acknowledged a vulnerability and are open. When we are open, we can receive. This is where creativity and higher knowledge will soon come forth. But during this state, it's of utmost importance to create the habits, posture, attitude, and openness of spirit to receive. This state is the unknown. And in the unknown, we settle in and adjust our sights to the darkness, our ears to the silence, and our body to the stillness.

But in this darkness, there is a luminosity, a brightness that begins to shine through. In the silence, there is a voice that begins to speak. And in the stillness, there is a newfound energy that begins to move you. But here's the key: It comes to you. You do not find it. That which you have been seeking is seeking you. It's coming because you're open. **So all this time, instead of you having to pray for it, you realize it has been praying for you – Source. You have been, and are being, created from this womb of powerlessness. Powerlessness is not weakness. It's not failure. It's not the end. It's the womb from which your new Self is born.** The ego fears this place because it knows it cannot survive here. And that's precisely why you must enter. Because what dies in powerlessness is not you, it's the false self, the controlling self, the small self that has kept you trapped. What emerges is something far greater. Something you could never have manufactured or controlled into being. Something that can only be received. **So when you find yourself powerless and you've exhausted all your strategies, when you've run out of answers, and when you finally say "I don't know"—don't flinch, instead stay. You're exactly where you need to be. You're in the womb. You're in the darkness before the dawn. You're only hearing silence before hearing the voice.** This module will help you sit in the unknown, embrace the waiting, and let go of the old self. The promise is that the light is coming, the voice is speaking, the energy is moving. And it's not coming because you earned it or figured it out or controlled your way to it. It's coming because you're loved beyond what you can imagine, and you finally stopped trying to create your own solution. This is the paradox: In powerlessness, you find power. In darkness, you find light. In silence, you hear the voice. In stillness, you find movement. Not by seeking, but by being sought. Not by finding, but by being found. Your only task is to trust the womb.

Mod 9 // Day 1

Reading

There is an innate desire to be in control and have a sense of where I am going. I want to know and when I don't, the state of powerlessness kicks in. Here I find I have two basic options, and neither feels good: I can make the decision myself but those around me often don't like it. It's usually done from a place of ruminating, figuring, controlling, manufacturing what I sense is best. Or I can capitulate, and go with the other person's decision and try to let go. But something in me doesn't feel at ease. This doesn't feel like true surrender either. I'm still frustrated. To be with powerlessness, from my initial urgent sense, feels like a painful stalemate. My mind fixates and wants a solution. I am prone to force one: make something happen, resolve the tension, escape the discomfort. To sit, wait, and listen doesn't feel natural. It feels painful. Until I practice it. **Until I sit, breathe, and become willing to see and hear this differently. When I do, I open myself up to the possibility of a third way. The first way is to control and try to make it happen. The second way is to fake it and go along halfheartedly, resentful beneath the surface. The third way is co-creating, with the other person, and with my Higher Power.** This is the way into the Larger Self by listening, trusting, and allowing something wiser than the ego to lead. New options begin to emerge, and we find ourselves going with rather than against. We are in flow with something inside us and in flow with others around us. Because we are no longer living from separation. I have found that asking this question makes a big difference in accessing this third way: **"How can I get creative here?"**

Journaling

What am I believing and experiencing today (emotionally, physically and spiritually)? What is my positive mindset and my negative mindset? How can I reparent myself with my current situation? What would the voice of Love say?

____

____

____

____

____

____

____

____

Vision

Reconnect to your Vision // What structure and implemenation needs to occur today?

____

____

Meditation

Dawnos *Air* Album // Track 5 – Space

Affirmation

Morning Affirmation _______________________________   Evening Affirmation _______________________________

Pausing   (Write out the times // set alarms)

Morning _____________   Midday _____________   Afternoon _____________   Evening _____________

Physical Movement

Walking, Yoga, Running, Weight lifting, Stretching, Jiu Jitsu, Pilates, or another: _______________

Resistance (Tasks for the Day)

Creative ____

Professional ____

Relationship(s) ____

Self ____

Evening Review

How did it go? What lesson(s) did I learn? Who do I need to make an amends with or forgive?

____

____

Reading

Whenever your confused and feel off, it's an indicator that you could have consciously, but more often unconsciously, subscribed to a negative belief. When this happens, it's time to go into the cave and wait for the light, which is truth. And often, you will experience a state of powerlessness as you enter this cave searching for the light. Now, oddly and paradoxically, as you enter into this cave of awareness, of existence, it's like there is a series of light switches that are to be turned on. But these switches are often different each time you enter. Meaning there's no formula for this because you and I are not in control, at least not from the ego state. **Instead, you enter with a single focus: finding the light and allowing the light to find you—truth and love. This is a paradox: the already and the not yet; the searching and the waiting; the asking and the receiving; the turning on and the turning off; the reaching and the letting go; the working and the resting; the asking and the listening.** And ultimately, you arrive at Source, and Source arrives to meet you. It's this mysterious dance that occurs, of seeming contradictions, only to experience that the light is both inside you and outside you.

In states of meditation, many people describe different experiences. For some, it is a deep sense of calm. Others speak of seeing colors or a gentle light. For others still, it shows up as a quiet sense of okayness, accompanied by warmth. What is equally wonderful, and also challenging, is that there is no formula for returning to it. There is no switch you can flip. When we try to control the experience or summon it on our own terms, it often slips away. And yet, this does not mean it is gone. It simply reminds us that this cave is only a cave to the ego mind. In truth, the peace, the voice, and the light are always present. We just do not always perceive them. And when we do, we remember again that we are already home.

Journaling

What am I believing and experiencing today (emotionally, physically and spiritually)? What is my positive mindset and my negative mindset? How can I reparent myself with my current situation? What would the voice of Love say?

Vision

Reconnect to your Vision // What structure and implemenation needs to occur today?

____

____

Meditation

Dawnos _Reoriented_ Album // Track 1 – Shadow Boxing

Affirmation

Morning Affirmation _______________________________   Evening Affirmation _______________________________

Pausing (Write out the times // set alarms)

Morning _____________   Midday _____________   Afternoon _____________   Evening _____________

Physical Movement

Walking, Yoga, Running, Weight lifting, Stretching, Jiu Jitsu, Pilates, or another: _______________

Resistance (Tasks for the Day)

Creative ____

Professional ____

Relationship(s) ____

Self ____

Evening Review

How did it go? What lesson(s) did I learn? Who do I need to make an amends with or forgive?

____

____

Reading

In this state of powerlessness, you may find yourself waking up to the day in front of you, often very aware of the loss of the world you once had. Maybe it's the loss of a loved one, or a job. Maybe you're dealing with pain in the body. The doorway through is a radical acceptance of the day and the situation in front of you. In this acceptance, in the acknowledgment that "it is what it is", you're no longer fighting against reality. You're going with it. And then you're allowing yourself to be on a course that is directing you toward something, not limited to what you can understand in your finite mind, but something beyond that. Because when there's no resistance, there's no frustration and friction. You've given yourself over to a higher purpose. It is truly living out "Thy will be done." This is the great act of faith, the lived expression of trust. It is trusting the flow of life is leading to your good and your benefit, though you cannot understand it. I can certainly tell you that there have been many, many moments where I have resisted and fought against what was happening. Life unfolded in ways where, at the time in my finite understanding, I thought it was the worst thing that could happen. And I fought against it. Honestly, I fought too long, which was unnecessary suffering.

But I look back at those very moments that I resisted so much, and I can honestly say the most painful events—I am at peace with what happened. Because I can see that the very thing I fought against was the very thing that brought a whole new turn of events that I couldn't have possibly comprehended at the time. This is the mystery of radical acceptance. You're not being asked to like what's happening. When you fight against what is, you're at war with reality itself. And reality always wins. But when you accept what is, when you surrender to the flow, you open yourself to something beyond your understanding. You make space for grace. You allow life to redirect you toward something for you not against you. And while you can't see it yet. But one day, you'll look back and understand.

Journaling

What am I believing and experiencing today (emotionally, physically and spiritually)? What is my positive mindset and my negative mindset? How can I reparent myself with my current situation? What would the voice of Love say?

____

____

____

____

____

____

Vision

Reconnect to your Vision // What structure and implemenation needs to occur today?

____

____

Meditation

Dawnos _Disoriented_ Album // Track 12 – Smile

Affirmation

Morning Affirmation _______________________________   Evening Affirmation _______________________________

Pausing (Write out the times // set alarms)

Morning _____________   Midday _____________   Afternoon _____________   Evening _____________

Physical Movement

Walking, Yoga, Running, Weight lifting, Stretching, Jiu Jitsu, Pilates, or another: _______________

Resistance (Tasks for the Day)

Creative ____

Professional ____

Relationship(s) ____

Self ____

Evening Review

How did it go? What lesson(s) did I learn? Who do I need to make an amends with or forgive?

____

____

Mod 9 // Day 4

Reading

During the lulls of life, those days and seasons of waiting, we are often prone to staying busy to fill the space or numbing out to avoid the emptiness. And yet, paradoxically, the gold is found in that very emptiness, in the void. The more we are willing to be with it, to enter its sacredness, the more it begins to change. What once felt like emptiness slowly reveals itself as spaciousness. The place we once avoided becomes something else entirely. It begins to feel like home. This experience can be deeply tranquil, but entering it often requires stillness and a willingness to allow emotions to dissolve rather than resist them. When you become still and pause, the goal is not to stop your thoughts. The goal is simply to notice, to be present, to be with what is.

I've found the OPEN tool is a particularly helpful tool in these moments. **O** is for *observe*: noticing what you are feeling and thinking. **P** is for *permission*: allowing what is present to be here without trying to change it. **E** is for *explore*: gently inquiring into the felt sense and experience what is. Is there an age associated with it? How old do you feel when this experience arises? Is there a color, a weight, a location in the body, or an image or symbol that represents it? This exploration is typically done meditatively, often with the eyes closed. Finally, **N** is for *nurture*: offering grace, care, and compassion to yourself. It is the act of meeting what you find with kindness rather than judgment.

I invite you to use this tool as a way of navigating these spaces—to move toward the void rather than away from it, and to discover what is waiting there.

Journaling

What am I believing and experiencing today (emotionally, physically and spiritually)? What is my positive mindset and my negative mindset? How can I reparent myself with my current situation? What would the voice of Love say?

____

____

____

____

____

____

____

Vision

Reconnect to your Vision // What structure and implemenation needs to occur today?

____

____

Meditation

Dawnos *Reoriented* Album // Track 2 – OPEN

Affirmation

Morning Affirmation ______________________________   Evening Affirmation ______________________________

Pausing (Write out the times // set alarms)

Morning ______________   Midday ______________   Afternoon ______________   Evening ______________

Physical Movement

Walking, Yoga, Running, Weight lifting, Stretching, Jiu Jitsu, Pilates, or another: ______________

Resistance (Tasks for the Day)

Creative ____

Professional ____

Relationship(s) ____

Self ____

Evening Review

How did it go? What lesson(s) did I learn? Who do I need to make an amends with or forgive?

____

____

Reading

Here's a common issue that keeps showing up: the pull to grasp for certainty instead of staying in the unknown. When we begin to embrace the unknown, there will almost always be resistance. Resistance to not having a plan. Resistance to not having a solution. Resistance to not having some guarantee that life is going to be okay. We want reassurance. We want certainty. We want guarantees. But the reality is that life already is okay, by being in this moment. Not the moment we are trying to control or manage or manufacture, but the moment that is actually here. This life, the one we are in right now. And in this moment, we already have everything we need. We already have access to Source. We already have access to wisdom, to presence, to something deeper than the mind's constant need to figure it all out. The lie we've been taught is that there is some missing piece. That there is some information, knowledge, or experience in the future that we believe we still need before we can arrive, be at peace, and be okay. And so we keep reaching ahead of ourselves, trying to know what can't yet be known. But the truth is that the willingness to stay in this moment of not knowing is what actually opens us. It creates space. It invites something larger than what we can understand from this finite perspective to meet us here.

So try this: radically accept this moment of "I don't know." Don't rush past it. It may feel uncomfortable and that's okay. Stay with it anyway. Let the discomfort be here without needing to fix it or resolve it. And rather than fighting this experience by shadowboxing with the unknown, be determined to see it differently. See it not as something to defeat, but as a teacher, even as a friend. Here's the promise: the unknown doesn't mean something has gone wrong. The unknown simply means new territory. It means a new frontier of expansion. And when you give yourself to it and you stop resisting and allow yourself to be here, awareness begins to arise. Awareness of what you couldn't see before. Awareness of what you couldn't know before.

Journaling

What am I believing and experiencing today (emotionally, physically and spiritually)? What is my positive mindset and my negative mindset? How can I reparent myself with my current situation? What would the voice of Love say?

____

____

____

____

____

____

Vision

Reconnect to your Vision // What structure and implemenation needs to occur today?

____

____

Meditation

Dawnos *Reoriented* Album // Track 1 – Unknown

Affirmation

Morning Affirmation _____________________________   Evening Affirmation _____________________________

Pausing   (Write out the times // set alarms)

Morning _____________   Midday _____________   Afternoon _____________   Evening _____________

Physical Movement

Walking, Yoga, Running, Weight lifting, Stretching, Jiu Jitsu, Pilates, or another: _______________

Resistance (Tasks for the Day)

Creative ____

Professional ____

Relationship(s) ____

Self ____

Evening Review

How did it go? What lesson(s) did I learn? Who do I need to make an amends with or forgive?

____

____

Reading

On New Year's Eve, my wife and I have a tradition with some of our best friends. Each year, the four of us reflect on the year behind us and set intentions for the year ahead. We've done this for several years now, and it has become a grounding ritual. This year, our friends shared a metaphor that landed deeply: the chrysalis. After dinner, they spoke about the stage between caterpillar and butterfly. The chrysalis phase and how powerfully it mirrors our own lives. It is a liminal space where transformation is actively happening, yet nothing appears to be happening at all. That paradoxical moment where it feels like nothing is happening and everything is happening at the same time.

The chrysalis is a cosmetic upgrade. The caterpillar doesn't get renovated into something slightly better. **What emerges is not an improved version of the old form, but something entirely new. A reconstitution into a larger self.** But first, it is dissolved and becomes biological mush. Then the process within the cocoon is set in motion. What's most astonishing is this: Inside the chrysalis, the wings already exist before the butterfly has any capacity to use them. And when the butterfly begins to emerge, there is struggle and real effort. That struggle is not accidental or cruel. It is essential and functional. Without it, the wings would never strengthen enough to function. When the butterfly finally breaks free, its wings are crumpled and fragile. It does not fly immediately and must wait. The wings slowly expand, dry, and harden. This waiting period is critical and vulnerable. The butterfly is exposed to the elements, exposed to predators. Stillness here is not optional; it is necessary. Only after this quiet strengthening does the butterfly take its first flight. And that first flight is often small and modest. But it changes everything. Orientation shifts and identity stabilizes. The butterfly is no longer what it was because it cannot return to the caterpillar life even if it wanted to.

Dissolution precedes design. The blueprint exists before the old form lets go. The struggle is functional, not punitive. The wings appear before the confidence to fly. Stillness is part of becoming capable. And the first flight, however small reorients everything. Now think about the parallel in your own life. Think about what it means to step into your larger self after a season of powerlessness. Think about how often we mistake the chrysalis for failure, stagnation, or regression; when in reality, it is the most creative phase of all.

Journaling

What am I believing and experiencing today (emotionally, physically and spiritually)? What is my positive mindset and my negative mindset? How can I reparent myself with my current situation? What would the voice of Love say?

____

____

____

____

____

Vision

Reconnect to your Vision // What structure and implemenation needs to occur today?

____

____

Meditation

Dawnos Diso*riented* Album // Track 11 – Cocoon

Affirmation

Morning Affirmation ____________________________   Evening Affirmation ________________________________

Pausing   **(Write out the times // set alarms)**

Morning _____________   Midday _____________   Afternoon _____________   Evening _____________

Physical Movement

Walking, Yoga, Running, Weight lifting, Stretching, Jiu Jitsu, Pilates, or another: _______________

Resistance (Tasks for the Day)

Creative ____

Professional ____

Relationship(s) ____

Self ____

Evening Review

How did it go? What lesson(s) did I learn? Who do I need to make an amends with or forgive?

____

____

Reading

Something truly happens when we move from the state of powerlessness into the state of the Larger Self that we will discuss in the next module. It is a confident surge of energy so strong that it overrides fear. There's a knowing that doesn't need convincing. Because when you know, you know. It comes from the gut, from the body. And it's hard to describe. There is this deep knowing that feels like it's coming from within, but it's equally coming from another place. "A knowing that knows". And from this place, it's not only confidence, it's a surge of joy. **Both childlike wonder and warrior-like strength. Both are needed. This is living in the middle. And the tension of the opposites no longer poses tension when you are in balance.** Here's the key: that vision, and specifically the voice coming from the mind of Love, will steady you. It not only centers you, it calms you. It calms that circus act fear tries to project inside your head. But when we settle in and open our heart, along with our inner sight and inner listening, we truly can see and hear. And I want to be very clear about what I'm saying here. This is not false positivity or empty promises. Your vision is *your* vision to fulfill.

What I seek to share is this: live a slow, steady, focused life rooted in truth and love, in service to your vision and your unique mission given by Source, and you will not fail. How can you, when you are a co-creator? When you step into the Larger Self, align with Source, and faithfully serve the vision you've been given, failure is not possible. Not because everything will go according to plan, but because you are living from expansion. You are living from alignment. You are living from the truth of who you are. This is not a guarantee of external success. It is a guarantee of internal integrity and fulfillment.

Journaling

What am I believing and experiencing today (emotionally, physically and spiritually)? What is my positive mindset and my negative mindset? How can I reparent myself with my current situation? What would the voice of Love say?

____

____

____

____

____

____

____

Vision

Reconnect to your Vision // What structure and implemenation needs to occur today?

____

____

Meditation

Dawnos *Disoriented* Album // Track 6 – Capacity

Affirmation

Morning Affirmation ______________________________   Evening Affirmation ________________________________

Pausing   (Write out the times // set alarms)

Morning _____________   Midday _____________   Afternoon _____________   Evening _____________

Physical Movement

Walking, Yoga, Running, Weight lifting, Stretching, Jiu Jitsu, Pilates, or another: _______________

Resistance (Tasks for the Day)

Creative ____

Professional ____

Relationship(s) ____

Self ____

Evening Review

How did it go? What lesson(s) did I learn? Who do I need to make an amends with or forgive?

____

____

Notes:

Ten

Larger Self

Here is the beautiful and profound truth, and I cannot emphasize this enough: all of us already have everything we need. The impulse to go outside of ourselves, to look for wisdom or knowledge from an authority figure, no longer holds the same power over us, because we are beginning to recognize that the knowing already exists within. Through the experience of powerlessness, something important has happened. By giving ourselves over to this state, we have discovered that there is a Voice within us that arises—a steady, loving voice. This is the beauty of it: a knowing that we can now begin to trust. Much of our culture and many religious structures have told us the opposite. They suggest that we are inherently bad, that we cannot trust ourselves, and that if we follow what we truly desire, it will lead us to destruction. The message has often been that safety comes from obedience to external authority, not from inner listening. But the reality is this: we are meant to trust ourselves. Who else could we follow? If we are not listening to the Spirit within us, then whose voice are we living by? This does not mean that we reject counsel or disconnect from those around us. It does not mean that we stop listening, learning, or being in relationship. But there is an important distinction here. If we are following someone else's voice, someone else's direction, then we are walking their path, not our own.

This is why the entrance into the state of the Larger Self matters so deeply. **If there is one essential idea I want to emphasize throughout this module, it is this: you can begin to trust and listen to you. No one else can live your life.** No one else can walk the path that is uniquely yours. When you begin to trust this inner, loving voice, the mind of Love, it will start to guide you. It will lead you toward the fulfillment of your own path. And that path is one of expansion: a widening, a deepening, a greater sense of aliveness and purpose. At this stage, the journey is no longer just about hearing the voice of Love or noticing what it is showing you. Now, the invitation is to follow it. This can be uncomfortable at first. Often, this voice leads toward change—toward letting go of familiar identities, structures, or attachments. Fear may arise, and with it the worry that trusting yourself will lead to harm or self-sabotage. It's not uncommon for people to experience this fear almost metaphorically, like being afraid that if you truly trusted yourself, you would somehow "fly the plane of your life into the ground," putting yourself and those you love at risk. But the irony is that staying small is what actually leads to destruction. What we often discover is that this deeper path is not leading us toward harm at all. It is leading us toward safety, even if it doesn't feel that way at first. The current we are moving into is not working against us, it is carrying us. And so the work now becomes learning to trust yourself. To trust that at your essence, you are good. That you are oriented toward love, not destruction. That you are worthy of being trusted. This is what this module will help you practice: trusting the voice within, following where it leads, and discovering that you are not only safe but can thrive with purpose.

Mod 10 // Day 1

Reading

There's an insightful metaphor that describes the state of our development and consciousness. This analogy comes from both Gurdjieff and, ultimately, Plato. I call it the horse-carriage-driver model. Here's how I understand it: First, notice all your desires, passions, emotions, and energy that you naturally hold. These instincts represent **the horse**. Then you have **the carriage**, which is your physical body. It represents your habits, your behaviors, your conditioning, and your biological limits and strengths. Next is **the driver**: the mind. This is your perceptions, your decision-making, your story. Basically, it's how you interpret reality. If the driver is asleep, the horse leads the carriage wherever it wants. This is the smaller self.

But behind the driver is a passenger: **the master**. The master will never force control, but is available if called upon. If given room and space, it will lead if allowed. This master is kind and loving, never dominant or domineering. This is our true self, the Larger Self. It's our soul, the inner witness. The tragedy is that before waking up, the driver never allows the master to lead. So in essence, life is void of direction, purpose, and fulfillment. It's often an abrupt change or turn of events that brings forth a redirection, an invitation to align with the master and the master's plan. But this is hard for the smaller self. In essence, if the driver doesn't check in, wake up, and allow the master to lead, the horse (emotions, passions, instincts) will run things. And the carriage (the body) will suffer the consequences, a simple cause and effect. Therefore, "the work" is to wake up, see, listen, follow, and trust.

Journaling

What am I believing and experiencing today (emotionally, physically and spiritually)? What is my positive mindset and my negative mindset? How can I reparent myself with my current situation? What would the voice of Love say?

____

____

____

____

____

____

____

____

Vision

Reconnect to your Vision // What structure and implemenation needs to occur today?

____

____

Meditation

Dawnos _Reoriented_ Album // Track 5 – New View

Affirmation

Morning Affirmation ______________________________   Evening Affirmation ______________________________

Pausing   (Write out the times // set alarms)

Morning _____________   Midday _____________   Afternoon _____________   Evening _____________

Physical Movement

Walking, Yoga, Running, Weight lifting, Stretching, Jiu Jitsu, Pilates, or another: _______________

Resistance (Tasks for the Day)

Creative ____

Professional ____

Relationship(s) ____

Self ____

Evening Review

How did it go? What lesson(s) did I learn? Who do I need to make an amends with or forgive?

____

____

Mod 10 // Day 2

Reading

As I wake up, I notice a familiar undercurrent: negative energy, fear, resentment, and, more than anything, old grievances toward myself. Beneath it all is a deep, ancient feeling: *I am not enough.* But when I slow down and really see this part of me, something softens. I feel compassion. I can even smile. This is my second-grade self—the boy who first learned to doubt himself. So much of who I am today, both the struggle and the strength, grew from this place. It is this same part of me that wakes me at 4:45 each morning, driven to fulfill a vision I have carried for years. If it weren't for my difficulties with school, with reading, with dyslexia, I don't know if that drive would exist in quite the same way. This place holds both determination and insecurity. It still longs for reassurance, that the vision will work, that the path is true. There have been times when following what was right in front of me felt wild, even reckless: living on 100% commission in commercial real estate, returning to graduate school twice, answering deeper callings that required trust and surrender. And yet, when I look back, it has always worked out. More than that, each time I followed the deeper pull within me, it led to expansion.

Through these life pivots, I've learned this: when I go with the flow, when I trust what my deeper self is calling me toward, life carries me. When I hesitate, when I cling to control, I struggle. It's like standing in a flowing stream. The moment I grab the edge, the water presses against me. When I let go, it moves with me. So today, I invite you to do the same. Return to the most painful place within you. Meet it with compassion and offer encouragement to yourself. **Trust this truth: not only will it work out—it will fully expand you, if you give yourself over to the process.** Now, access your deepest and highest self. Imagine yourself at eighty years old. What would your eighty-year-old self say to you today? Write it down. Let this become your affirmation.

Journaling

What am I believing and experiencing today (emotionally, physically and spiritually)? What is my positive mindset and my negative mindset? How can I reparent myself with my current situation? What would the voice of Love say?

____

____

____

____

____

____

Vision

Reconnect to your Vision // What structure and implemenation needs to occur today?

____

____

Meditation

Dawnos *Oriented* Album // Track 12 – Energy Grid

Affirmation

Morning Affirmation ______________________________   Evening Affirmation ______________________________

Pausing   (Write out the times // set alarms)

Morning ______________   Midday ______________   Afternoon ______________   Evening ______________

Physical Movement

Walking, Yoga, Running, Weight lifting, Stretching, Jiu Jitsu, Pilates, or another: ______________

Resistance (Tasks for the Day)

Creative ____

Professional ____

Relationship(s) ____

Self ____

Evening Review

How did it go? What lesson(s) did I learn? Who do I need to make an amends with or forgive?

____

____

Mod 10 // Day 3

Reading

When we encounter a direct situation or circumstance that seems to assault us, sometimes even paralyze us with fear and shame, it often disguises itself as rational thinking, false self-motivation, or harsh inner criticism. This is fear in its counterfeit form, and beneath it, shame in disguise. Yet this moment is not a failure; it is an invitation. An opportunity to look directly at what we have been avoiding and to see it in a new way. By facing it rather than fleeing it, we loosen its power and begin to free ourselves from it.

As Joseph Campbell reminds us, the dragon we are trying to slay is often ourselves. When we finally turn toward this metaphorical dragon, **we discover it is not an enemy to destroy, but a lost part of us asking to be brought home.** This is a universal myth for every man and woman. It echoes the familiar childhood story of the monster in the closet: terrifying in the dark, yet revealed in the light to be far less dangerous than imagined, sometimes even afraid of us. This myth maps the stages of the hero's journey we all must walk. First, there is the recognition that fear and shame are normal, part of being human. Then comes engagement: choosing to listen, to stay, to sit with what arises rather than pushing it away. We don't just hear it; we allow ourselves to understand it. From there, transformation becomes possible.

This arc is at the heart of the **HOPE** practice: **H — Humanity** (this is part of being human), **O — Open** (stay present and receptive), **P — Peace** (allow softening rather than resistance), **E — Everything** (nothing is excluded)

It is within this final stage—*Everything*—that integration occurs. Here, the inner and outer worlds meet. This is what Campbell called the "mastery of the two worlds," the culminating phase of the monomyth. It is a stage marked not by bravado, but by freedom, because when we no longer avoid what we fear, even death itself loses its grip.

Journaling

What am I believing and experiencing today (emotionally, physically and spiritually)? What is my positive mindset and my negative mindset? How can I reparent myself with my current situation? What would the voice of Love say?

____

____

____

____

____

____

Vision

Reconnect to your Vision // What structure and implemenation needs to occur today?

____

____

Meditation

Dawnos _Reoriented_ Album // Track 6 – HOPE

Affirmation

Morning Affirmation _______________________________   Evening Affirmation _______________________________

Pausing   (Write out the times // set alarms)

Morning _____________   Midday _____________   Afternoon _____________   Evening _____________

Physical Movement

Walking, Yoga, Running, Weight lifting, Stretching, Jiu Jitsu, Pilates, or another: _______________

Resistance (Tasks for the Day)

Creative ____

Professional ____

Relationship(s) ____

Self ____

Evening Review

How did it go? What lesson(s) did I learn? Who do I need to make an amends with or forgive?

____

____

Reading

A while back, I had a decision I needed to make, one that required several days of discernment. Ultimately, it was a decision that not everyone would be happy with. There were people close to me who would be disappointed. Some questioned me and challenged me with their own concerns and fears. It felt very weighty. But each morning, as I would journal, pray, and meditate, the voice of Love kept assuring me to go with my gut, that it would be okay to make the decision I truly wanted to make. And so I did. Ultimately, everything worked out beautifully, just as I sensed it would, though it was definitely uncomfortable along the way. The background of the following passage comes from a recording I made while out on a run. This is nearly verbatim what I recorded to myself as a form of encouragement. I hope it encourages you as well. Later, I recorded this as a meditation called *Believe*.

When you're challenged, see it as a gift. Yes, fear shows up: in the form of images and language. This fear will try to challenge the direct vision and path you are on. See it as a gift. It may come in the form of those closest to you, and in their state of fear, they may not believe it—because of their own fear. My friend, see through it. This is the doorway past the upper ceiling. When you're challenged, hone in on truth. Hone in on what's real, what you know. It's a gift to help you anchor down in that deeper knowing. And so, **we all have a choice right here: to see through it, to see Heaven or Hell. Heaven is that truth: that knowing within us.** And with it, it does require something, that something is belief. To believe in that truth. To believe that you have it in yourself to hold to it. And then you're in flow. Then you anchor into it, and you go with it. So then, those around you, see their fear and send love back to them. Go and send love to them. And send love to yourself, to the parts of you that still don't believe it. So when you're challenged, anchor into what's true. Bring to mind this verse: *Trust in the Lord with all your heart, and lean not on your own understanding; but in all your ways acknowledge Him, which is Source, and Source will make your path straight.* Trust in the law (the law means truth). Trust in the law with all your heart and lean not on your own understanding (ego). And in all your ways—which means all your daily movements, daily responsibilities, daily thoughts—acknowledge Source, and Source will make your paths straight. This is it. You got it.

Journaling

What am I believing and experiencing today (emotionally, physically and spiritually)? What is my positive mindset and my negative mindset? How can I reparent myself with my current situation? What would the voice of Love say?

____

____

____

____

____

Vision

Reconnect to your Vision // What structure and implemenation needs to occur today?

____

____

Meditation

Dawnos – Outside the Sky // Track – Believe

Affirmation

Morning Affirmation _______________________________   Evening Affirmation _______________________________

Pausing   (Write out the times // set alarms)

Morning _____________   Midday _____________   Afternoon _____________   Evening _____________

Physical Movement

Walking, Yoga, Running, Weight lifting, Stretching, Jiu Jitsu, Pilates, or another: _______________

Resistance (Tasks for the Day)

Creative ____

Professional ____

Relationship(s) ____

Self ____

Evening Review

How did it go? What lesson(s) did I learn? Who do I need to make an amends with or forgive?

____

____

Mod 10 // Day 5

Reading

For many, the invitation to slow down and sit in silence can feel like torture, or simply a waste of time. I wish someone would have told me early on in my life, before I ever learned about meditation, that there is a simple and deeply helpful practice. It uses sound as a way to shift into the Larger Self, to move out of the smaller, limited viewpoint and into an open expanse. This practice is called the Cosmic Hum, and it works like this: you focus on all the sounds around you, the air conditioning, the birds, the cars outside. You invite them all in instead of excluding them. You listen to every sound without judgment or preference. Then, you shift your attention to a background sound, the one that is always with you. The ringing in your ears. This is known as the sound of silence, or the Cosmic Hum.

What is amazing, and incredibly effective, is that this practice helps you drop into the Larger Self almost immediately. As you focus on this background sound, something natural happens: the cosmic hum shifts to the foreground, and the normal sounds begin to fade to the background. You are no longer distracted by the noise of the world. You are listening to what has always been there, beneath it all. And here's what's remarkable: **this practice naturally slows your thinking mind and rumination softens. Your attention loosens from that limited reality, that narrow perspective.** Because you are so focused on the cosmic hum, presence arrives. It naturally eases you into stillness. This is not something you force. You don't have to fight your mind or wrestle your thoughts into submission. You simply shift your attention from the foreground to the background, from the noise to the silence that holds it all. In that shift, you arrive. You are no longer the Smaller Self caught in thoughts and worries. You are the awareness that hears it all: the Larger Self, the witness. So today, try this practice. Sit quietly and listen to the sounds around you, all of them. Then tune into the background sound, the ringing, the hum that is always there. Let it become the foreground. Let everything else fade. Notice what happens and how your thinking slows. Notice how you become present and how you naturally ease into the Larger Self.

Journaling

What am I believing and experiencing today (emotionally, physically and spiritually)? What is my positive mindset and my negative mindset? How can I reparent myself with my current situation? What would the voice of Love say?

Vision

Reconnect to your Vision // What structure and implemenation needs to occur today?

____

____

Meditation

Dawnos _Reoriented_ Album // Track 4 – Cosmic Hum

Affirmation

Morning Affirmation _______________________   Evening Affirmation _______________________

Pausing   (Write out the times // set alarms)

Morning ____________   Midday ____________   Afternoon ____________   Evening ____________

Physical Movement

Walking, Yoga, Running, Weight lifting, Stretching, Jiu Jitsu, Pilates, or another: ______________

Resistance (Tasks for the Day)

Creative ____

Professional ____

Relationship(s) ____

Self ____

Evening Review

How did it go? What lesson(s) did I learn? Who do I need to make an amends with or forgive?

____

____

Mod 10 // Day 6

Reading

To be of service, to be willing to live with a purpose bigger than just ourselves, requires openness. That is the starting point. **The soul seeks to expand: to grow love and light in you, and to extend it to those around you. When we return to this purpose, this vision, we come back into alignment.**

And here, the practice is simple and real: notice what's here: the thoughts, the emotions. The sensations in the body, what we call the ego body, are experienced as tightness and constriction. Bring awareness to it all without fighting it. Then gently shift your awareness toward love and light, the mind of Love. In essence, you take what normally sits in the foreground, thoughts, emotions, sensations, the mind of fear, and place it in the background.And you bring the background of awareness to the foreground. This shift to loving awareness is essential.

It's what every athlete, performer, and artist learns to access when they enter flow. More importantly, it is in the ordinary, practical moments of life, especially in relationships, that we learn how to bring compassion to whoever is in front of us. **This new view can be instantaneous.** An athlete on the field or the court doesn't have the luxury of disappearing into the mountains for a day or going on a retreat. So what does it look like for us, right here, in everyday life? When you are navigating your inner critic, fear, or shame, or when your relationships feel challenging, come back to this viewpoint of loving awareness. See from this place. Because when you do, everything shifts. You live, respond, and see differently.

Journaling

What am I believing and experiencing today (emotionally, physically and spiritually)? What is my positive mindset and my negative mindset? How can I reparent myself with my current situation? What would the voice of Love say?

____

____

____

____

____

____

____

____

Vision

Reconnect to your Vision // What structure and implemenation needs to occur today?

____

____

Meditation

Dawnos _Reoriented_ Album // Track 5 – New View

Affirmation

Morning Affirmation _______________________________   Evening Affirmation _______________________________

Pausing   (Write out the times // set alarms)

Morning _____________   Midday _____________   Afternoon _____________   Evening _____________

Physical Movement

Walking, Yoga, Running, Weight lifting, Stretching, Jiu Jitsu, Pilates, or another: _______________

Resistance (Tasks for the Day)

Creative ____

Professional ____

Relationship(s) ____

Self ____

Evening Review

How did it go? What lesson(s) did I learn? Who do I need to make an amends with or forgive?

____

____

Mod 10 // Day 7

Reading

By this point, you're over halfway through the twelve modules. Today is a good moment to pause: to stop, refocus, and return to The Vision, especially the vision statement you distilled into two to four sentences earlier in the "Establish Your Vision" section of this workbook.

Go back and reread your Vision statement. If it feels supportive, write it out again by hand. Then sit with it in silence for five minutes.

One practice I recommend is reading the statement aloud and recording it on your voice memo app. **Listen to your own voice speaking forth your vision, and then allow yourself to sit quietly afterward, simply listening.**

When you're ready, write back to yourself from the voice of Love: the most loving, encouraging voice within you. Don't edit or hold back. Let whatever wants to be said come through.

Journaling

What am I believing and experiencing today (emotionally, physically and spiritually)? What is my positive mindset and my negative mindset? How can I reparent myself with my current situation? What would the voice of Love say?

Vision

Reconnect to your Vision // What structure and implemenation needs to occur today?

____

____

Meditation

Dawnos _Oriented_ Album // Track 1 – Vision & Purpose

Affirmation

Morning Affirmation ____________________________   Evening Affirmation ______________________________

Pausing   (Write out the times // set alarms)

Morning _____________   Midday _____________   Afternoon _____________   Evening _____________

Physical Movement

Walking, Yoga, Running, Weight lifting, Stretching, Jiu Jitsu, Pilates, or another: _______________

Resistance (Tasks for the Day)

Creative ____

Professional ____

Relationship(s) ____

Self ____

Evening Review

How did it go? What lesson(s) did I learn? Who do I need to make an amends with or forgive?

____

____

Notes:

Eleven

Connection

I can still remember the first time I heard U2—particularly *The Joshua Tree* and *Achtung Baby*. Their sound has always moved me, and the song *One* has stayed with me. There may be no better song for this module on Connection. The idea for *One* emerged after the Dalai Lama invited U2 to play at an event called *The Festival of Oneness*. Bono declined the invitation, signing his letter, "Respectfully yours, Bono," and adding a postscript: "One, but not the same." Bono later explained that *One* is not about oneness in the sentimental sense. It's about difference. It's not the old hippie idea of "let's all live together." It's something much more punk rock, almost anti-romantic. "We are one, but we're not the same. We get to carry each other." It's a reminder, he said, that we don't really have a choice. An excerpt from *One* reads:

> *One love, one blood*
> *One life, you got to do what you should*
> *One life, with each other*
> *Sisters, brothers*
> *One life, but we're not the same⊠*
> *We get to carry each other, carry each other*
> *One*

And here is the paradox: difference and togetherness are not opposites. They belong together. This is what I often refer to as the Third Way, a path that holds tension without collapsing into extremes. In typical rock-and-roll fashion, there's something anarchic here: anti-establishment, skeptical of easy unity, and yet still insisting on connection. Even activism, disagreement, and resistance can share common ground across divisions: Republicans and Democrats, tribe beside tribe, Christians and Muslims, and those who claim none at all. Difference does not rule out love. Disagreement does not negate connection. Carrying one another does not require sameness. It's easy to love people who listen to the same music, hold the same religious beliefs, and share the same political views. But it's much harder to love someone when they vote for a different party, worship differently, or see the world through a completely different lens. Look at your own life and examine it honestly: how different and diverse are your friendships? Martin Luther King Jr. once said that the most segregated hour of the week is Sunday morning, and decades later, that observation still rings painfully true. This module is a call to love beyond what we already know. It invites us to look past our comfortable circles and recognize the common denominator we all share: our humanity and the truth that each of us bears the image of God. We are one, but we're not the same. And that's exactly the point.

Mod 11 // Day 1

Reading

This whole time, as you've been focusing on your own vision, its fulfillment, and its legitimacy, you discover something profound. Fulfilling your vision is no longer just about you. By this point, you have learned to see through the shadow, face the inner critic, and access your own inner strength by listening to the inner voice guiding you. **And here's the shift. In finding and fulfilling your vision, you realize you can now take it to those around you. You're able to help those closest to you, and people who come along your path, find their own vision.** This becomes an even greater joy because you're now giving back, mentoring and guiding others. Light shines upon light. This is how we illuminate the world.

Over the last few years, I've had this keen sense: part of my fulfillment was not only to realize this vision, but to live it out, experience it, and taste all the fruits of the vision so I could share this very practice with you and others around me. So that you too could fulfill your vision. These dreams that are deep within us aren't too wild. **There's a reason we have these dreams and visions. There's a reason they're very specific to you and your unique calling.** Your dreams will not be my dreams. Their uniqueness comes from you, your gifts, and how God has formed you. And all of this is connection. Because then we get to take what we have grown into and experienced, and share this knowing with everyone else. That they too can listen to the voice of Love. So as you've worked out your own vision, now allow yourself to see those around you and bring encouragement to them. Know that you are not only fulfilling yours, but you can take it to others. Because life is about expansion, and our fulfillment is to bring love and light to those we encounter. *When it's dark, the light must shine even brighter.* So remember: you're not alone. This vision is meant to be shared with others. This is the good news.

Journaling

What am I believing and experiencing today (emotionally, physically and spiritually)? What is my positive mindset and my negative mindset? How can I reparent myself with my current situation? What would the voice of Love say?

____

____

____

____

____

____

Vision

Reconnect to your Vision // What structure and implemenation needs to occur today?

____

____

Meditation

Dawnos *Air* Album // Track 6 – Rhythm

Affirmation

Morning Affirmation ____________________________   Evening Affirmation ______________________________________

Pausing (Write out the times // set alarms)

Morning ______________   Midday ______________   Afternoon ______________   Evening ______________

Physical Movement

Walking, Yoga, Running, Weight lifting, Stretching, Jiu Jitsu, Pilates, or another: ________________

Resistance (Tasks for the Day)

Creative ____

Professional ____

Relationship(s) ____

Self ____

Evening Review

How did it go? What lesson(s) did I learn? Who do I need to make an amends with or forgive?

____

____

____

Mod 11 // Day 2

Reading

How do we define success? From an ego standpoint, the smaller self, success is the accumulation of possessions, superiority, power, and climbing the ladder. This unconsciously creates more separation. It says, "I'm better than you." It's a treadmill that keeps you chasing a carrot we all know we can't take with us after death. It creates more separation. But from a deeper, soulful standpoint, we can't fully define success. It's something both outside of us and yet within us, an attending spirit. I intially heard this idea in Mark Nepo's Book of Awakening that the root of the word "genius" originally meant "attending spirit." In classical Roman times, genius referred to a protective guardian spirit that was external to the individual, not an internal quality. It wasn't until the mid-1700s that this meaning shifted, when exceptional people began to be called geniuses in their own right. **There is a mysterious link between something outside us and something within us, a connection to Source. And here's the key: we are to serve the work the genius calls forth.** We serve the voice. By doing so, we are in service to something bigger than ourselves. There's a modern example of this: Jay-Z earned the nickname "Hova" (short for "J-Hova," a play on Jehovah) back in 1993 when people in the studio marveled at his ability to improvise all his lyrics without writing them down. His ability seemed nothing short of miraculous. He was clear that he didn't want to offend anyone by calling himself God. 'I know better than that,' he said. Still, he wanted to recognize the gift he had. Something was moving through him that was beyond just him.

There are countless stories like this, artists and musicians sitting in a recording studio when something happens during the process of making the song. They can't claim it was necessarily them, nor can they recreate it on demand. But it's happening. They're listening and following. And they just know, something transcendent just occurred. But none of us really knows what it is. We don't know how it happens. So what is success, really? It's living out of the fullness of who you are. It's listening and being in flow. It's serving something greater. Success isn't something you achieve. It's something you align with. It's not about accumulating more or being better than others. It's about being present to what's moving through you and having the courage to follow it.

Journaling

What am I believing and experiencing today (emotionally, physically and spiritually)? What is my positive mindset and my negative mindset? How can I reparent myself with my current situation? What would the voice of Love say?

____

____

____

____

Vision

Reconnect to your Vision // What structure and implemenation needs to occur today?

____

____

Meditation

Dawnos _Oriented_ Album // Track 7 – SOURCE

Affirmation

Morning Affirmation ___________________________   Evening Affirmation ___________________________________

Pausing   (Write out the times // set alarms)

Morning ____________   Midday ____________   Afternoon ____________   Evening ____________

Physical Movement

Walking, Yoga, Running, Weight lifting, Stretching, Jiu Jitsu, Pilates, or another: _______________

Resistance (Tasks for the Day)

Creative ____

Professional ____

Relationship(s) ____

Self ____

Evening Review

How did it go? What lesson(s) did I learn? Who do I need to make an amends with or forgive?

____

____

____

Mod 11 // Day 3

Reading

There are times in life when you find yourself frustrated, holding resentment toward someone around you. Maybe it's your spouse, a friend, a family member, or a colleague. Or perhaps it's a person who is no longer part of your daily life, but still deeply bothers you. The reality is this: you and I are still connected to those people, and how we relate to them in our mind is how we relate to us and the world. It's all connected. The energy and thoughts we hold are what we send out to the world. Again, it's all connected. So when we can see them as a brother, a sister, or a friend, and allow ourselves to connect with them in love, we no longer mirror back darkness and separation. Here's a way to practice this: Picture a person that bothers you. Really see their face in your mind. Try to see them smiling. Then imagine a light above you, shining down on you. Allow it to fully illuminate you in such a way that it begins to shine forth from you. And this light radiates outward, shining on them. All the while, you're filled up with this light.

Remember that what you think, you make real. This applies to both light and dark. The call is to be free and to free those around you. And the moment you access this light, you see that we're all connected. There's an incredible warmth in this realization, but it requires fierce determination to want to see it differently. This is the great miracle: you can be the miracle. But it requires mastery. You will be challenged. The challenges will come forth. Yet with motivation and practice, you can master this. And when you do, you are providing the miracle to the other person. When you free them in your mind, you free yourself. When you shine light on them, you fill yourself with light. When you see them with love, you become love. This is not about condoning harmful behavior or pretending nothing happened. It's about releasing the grip that resentment has on you. It's about recognizing that holding onto darkness toward another person only keeps you in darkness. See them through the light. Let it shine on you both.

Journaling

What am I believing and experiencing today (emotionally, physically and spiritually)? What is my positive mindset and my negative mindset? How can I reparent myself with my current situation? What would the voice of Love say?

____

____

____

____

____

____

Vision

Reconnect to your Vision // What structure and implemenation needs to occur today?

____

____

Meditation

Dawnos *Oriented* Album // Track 9 – Healing Light

Affirmation

Morning Affirmation _______________________________   Evening Affirmation _______________________________

Pausing   (Write out the times // set alarms)

Morning _____________   Midday _____________   Afternoon _____________   Evening _____________

Physical Movement

Walking, Yoga, Running, Weight lifting, Stretching, Jiu Jitsu, Pilates, or another: _______________

Resistance (Tasks for the Day)

Creative ____

Professional ____

Relationship(s) ____

Self ____

Evening Review

How did it go? What lesson(s) did I learn? Who do I need to make an amends with or forgive?

____

____

____

Mod 11 // Day 4

Reading

There is an ancient meditation practice called Tonglen that centers on compassion. It's simple and direct, and when practiced, it works. **Tonglen begins by turning toward what's difficult.** Rather than avoiding conflict, discomfort, or painful emotions, the practice invites you to meet them honestly, without needing to fix or defend. It may be a situation you're facing, an emotion that's been lingering, or a story someone else holds about you during a moment of tension or conflict. You bring it into awareness through prayer, meditation, or simply as you go for a walk. On the in-breath, you take in what is present: the heaviness, the hurt, the shame, the guilt. You may also take in the other person's anger, blame, or accusation, along with your own reactions. You allow what's there to be acknowledged. On the out-breath, you offer love. You breathe out warmth, care, and compassion, first toward yourself, and then outward. You're not excusing harm or denying truth. You're creating space for something deeper to emerge.

As this rhythm continues, the heart begins to change. Tonglen has a way of clarifying things. It can reveal where responsibility is needed and where compassion has been missing. It helps us stay out of the victim role without turning against ourselves or others. What's true becomes clearer, and what isn't begins to loosen its grip. **At its core, this practice is about love, not as sentiment, but as a transforming force.** Love that can hold pain without being consumed by it. Love that knows how to move and heal. Tonglen isn't reserved for meditation cushions. It can be practiced in real time, even in the middle of an argument. You simply return to the breath, bring the person or situation into awareness, and choose to respond with love. This may appear gentle on the surface, but it requires real courage. It's an active form of forgiveness, one that doesn't bypass reality and doesn't abandon the self. And the end result is freedom.

Journaling

What am I believing and experiencing today (emotionally, physically and spiritually)? What is my positive mindset and my negative mindset? How can I reparent myself with my current situation? What would the voice of Love say?

Vision

Reconnect to your Vision // What structure and implemenation needs to occur today?

____

____

Meditation

Dawnos _Reoriented_ Album // Track 8 – Tonglen

Affirmation

Morning Affirmation ______________________________   Evening Affirmation ______________________________

Pausing   (Write out the times // set alarms)

Morning ______________   Midday ______________   Afternoon ______________   Evening ______________

Physical Movement

Walking, Yoga, Running, Weight lifting, Stretching, Jiu Jitsu, Pilates, or another: ______________

Resistance (Tasks for the Day)

Creative ____

Professional ____

Relationship(s) ____

Self ____

Evening Review

How did it go? What lesson(s) did I learn? Who do I need to make an amends with or forgive?

____

____

Reading

In this state of connection, there's a profound realization I want to communicate simply. It isn't the familiar idea of "we're all one," which can sound abstract or overly spiritualized, and frankly isn't that earth-shattering. While I believe that idea is true, the deeper shift lies in a movement from local consciousness to universal consciousness. Local consciousness carries the burden of separation: it assumes the responsibility is on us to have the knowledge, to figure it out, to make something happen. It's isolating, heavy, and effort-driven. Universal consciousness, by contrast, offers a larger perspective: one in which wisdom isn't something we manufacture but something we access.

This shift is deeply freeing. Instead of it being on us to hold all the answers, our role becomes much simpler: we raise the antenna. We stay connected. Richard Rohr refers to this as Christ consciousness, a **universal field of knowing that we participate in rather than control.** Modern technology offers a helpful metaphor here. Think of an iPhone: it has access to nearly all the information in the world, yet it isn't storing or carrying that information internally. It simply connects when needed. The power isn't in possession; it's in access. The same is true of consciousness. We don't have to download or hoard wisdom, we attune to it.

This reframes how we understand practice and learning. What we often call "muscle memory" is a misnomer. When we practice piano, tennis, or jiu-jitsu, we aren't forcing knowledge into the body through repetition alone. **We're refining our ability to tune in, to respond from a deeper intelligence that already knows. Practice becomes less about effort and more about alignment.** And this is precisely the point of the daily practices: not self-improvement through strain, but steady attunement to a larger awareness. Over time, we learn to recognize and trust that signal, to live, move, and choose from what we call the voice of Love.

Journaling

What am I believing and experiencing today (emotionally, physically and spiritually)? What is my positive mindset and my negative mindset? How can I reparent myself with my current situation? What would the voice of Love say?

____

____

____

____

____

____

Vision

Reconnect to your Vision // What structure and implemenation needs to occur today?

____

____

Meditation

Dawnos Reo*riented* Album // Track 4 – Cosmic Hum

Affirmation

Morning Affirmation ________________________________   Evening Affirmation ________________________________

Pausing   (Write out the times // set alarms)

Morning _____________   Midday _____________   Afternoon _____________   Evening _____________

Physical Movement

Walking, Yoga, Running, Weight lifting, Stretching, Jiu Jitsu, Pilates, or another: _______________

Resistance (Tasks for the Day)

Creative ____

Professional ____

Relationship(s) ____

Self ____

Evening Review

How did it go? What lesson(s) did I learn? Who do I need to make an amends with or forgive?

____

____

____

Reading

In the state of connection, which is not exclusive to a long life lived or to enlightened masters, we move from control to collaboration. This is a state, not just a stage. It is available to all of us now, in the present moment. Here, because we are connected and flowing, **we are in dialogue with life, not at war with it**. It's akin to having an antenna raised, tuned into a creative and ever-present communication, something like receiving a download. But this "download" is for the purpose of service, not for the ego's gain. From this place, life seems to answer back.

A story that emphasizes this involves Mary Oliver, one of my favorite and most acclaimed poets. The story goes that she was teaching someone about writing a poem, demonstrating a technical point and offering guidance. In the process of helping another, she unintentionally wrote one of her most famous poems, Wild Geese. Because she wasn't trying to make something great, she was simply writing and helping someone else. Because she was in service, this beautiful poem came into being.

There's no better way to summarize this reflection than to share the last few lines from her poem:

> Whoever you are, no matter how lonely,
> the world offers itself to your imagination,
> calls to you like the wild geese, harsh and exciting—
> over and over announcing your place
> in the family of things. ~ Mary Oliver, Wild Geese

Journaling

What am I believing and experiencing today (emotionally, physically and spiritually)? What is my positive mindset and my negative mindset? How can I reparent myself with my current situation? What would the voice of Love say?

____

____

____

____

____

____

Vision

Reconnect to your Vision // What structure and implemenation needs to occur today?

____

____

Meditation

Dawnos _Reoriented_ Album // Track 9 – Gratitude

Affirmation

Morning Affirmation _______________________   Evening Affirmation _______________________

Pausing   (Write out the times // set alarms)

Morning _____________   Midday _____________   Afternoon _____________   Evening _____________

Physical Movement

Walking, Yoga, Running, Weight lifting, Stretching, Jiu Jitsu, Pilates, or another: _______________

Resistance (Tasks for the Day)

Creative ____

Professional ____

Relationship(s) ____

Self ____

Evening Review

How did it go? What lesson(s) did I learn? Who do I need to make an amends with or forgive?

____

____

Mod 11 // Day 7

Reading

There's a difference between forcing and flowing. Between effort driven by ego and movement that comes from alignment. When you live from a place of connection, you stop trying to muscle your way through life. You stop forcing solutions. Instead, you move with what is—responsive, fluid, conserving energy for what matters. I've recently started training in jiu-jitsu again. It has always been a practice I've had great respect for, a martial art that is both beautiful and incredibly effective. Like any practice worth doing, jiu-jitsu requires years of training. The techniques, movements, and sequences seem almost unlimited. And when you start, it's like being dropped into the center of an ocean. It's incredibly confusing and vulnerable. What's fascinating about jiu-jitsu, and unusual for a combat sport, is that practitioners can still train and compete in their 50s and 60s. This is because jiu-jitsu isn't about brute strength. It's about efficiency, leverage, and technique. When you watch a white belt roll, they expend enormous energy, thrashing, forcing, gripping with everything they have. They're exhausted within minutes. But when you watch a black belt, someone who has been training for years, they hardly exert energy at all. They are at ease. Their movements have an almost peaceful, anaconda-like quality, fluid and effortless. Their experience has shown them how to conserve energy and find alignment while the other person spends theirs. When the other person makes a mistake, as they always do, the black belt finds it, capitalizes on it, and moves toward a submission.

This is what living from a state of connection looks like. **In the state of connection, you are at ease and in flow. You are no longer forcing solutions. You are no longer thrashing through life, exhausting yourself with effort that comes from fear or the need to prove something. Instead, you move with awareness. You conserve your energy. You wait and then respond.** And when the opening appears, you act clarity instead of urgency. As Bruce Lee said: "Be water, my friend." Water doesn't force. It flows, it adapts, and finds the path of least resistance. And over time, it shapes mountains. This is the invitation of wholeness: to stop forcing and start flowing. To trust that when you're aligned—with yourself, with Source, with what is—the right movement will emerge. Not through effort, but through patience, practice, and awareness. So today, notice where you're forcing. Where you're exhausting yourself trying to make something happen. And remember: be water, my friend.

Journaling

What am I believing and experiencing today (emotionally, physically and spiritually)? What is my positive mindset and my negative mindset? How can I reparent myself with my current situation? What would the voice of Love say?

____

____

____

____

____

Vision

Reconnect to your Vision // What structure and implemenation needs to occur today?

____

____

Meditation

Dawnos *Reoriented* Album // Track 7 – Flow

Affirmation

Morning Affirmation ______________________________   Evening Affirmation ______________________________

Pausing (Write out the times // set alarms)

Morning _____________   Midday _____________   Afternoon _____________   Evening _____________

Physical Movement

Walking, Yoga, Running, Weight lifting, Stretching, Jiu Jitsu, Pilates, or another: _______________

Resistance (Tasks for the Day)

Creative ____

Professional ____

Relationship(s) ____

Self ____

Evening Review

How did it go? What lesson(s) did I learn? Who do I need to make an amends with or forgive?

____

____

Notes:

Twelve

Wholeness

As we arrive at this final module on wholeness, we come full circle to where we began, with the co-creative state, a second innocence. Our hope, and really our mission, is that we each integrate the inner child and the various parts of the ego, so that we not only recognize our wholeness but begin to live from it. **Wholeness means living from a state of abundance rather than lack. It means you no longer seek something outside yourself to complete you, because you recognize that you already have it all.** Remember the earlier metaphor from Gurdjieff: you are now the master in the carriage. You are no longer controlled by the emotions, the horse; no longer driven by unconscious behaviors, the carriage; and no longer over-identified with the thoughts of the mind, the driver. Instead, you live from the witness, while also having the capacity to consciously assume your role, what Carl Jung would call your own kingship. Jung spoke often of archetypal energies, and this is the kingly role: all parts working together, in harmony and in flow. Not flow for its own sake, but flow that allows you to participate in the fulfillment of your own destiny. **The great lie is that we are completely fated by some harsh, cosmic force—that we have no say, that we are merely victims of circumstance. But the truth is more relational than that. We collaborate because if we are all one, does that not also mean one with Source?** And if so, does it not follow that we too have the capacity to co-create with Source? A beautiful dance of listening and speaking, questioning and responding—all in service of fulfillment. A quiet mission to love, and to spread the good news that those around us, too, can create from abundance rather than fear. What if the thing you most deeply want is already within reach? What if it has been waiting for you to become whole enough to receive it?

Jacob wrestling with the angel, refusing to let go until he was blessed, was not a battle with something external. It was Jacob wrestling with himself: ego and spirit. And the merging of the two was the blessing. The fulfillment and the unfolding of wholeness. This has been my experience. And it's why I want to pass this on to you. **If something is truly of the Spirit, it is not only possible, it is viable. It is ready to be lived.** That vision you have been sitting with, meditating on, has already gone through a deep process of discernment. And now, it is essential to return to what you've been carrying. The vision you wrote down. The one that took courage just to name. The one that felt silly, wild, or even reckless at moments. The vision that may have been too embarrassing to share with others, or too risky to fully allow yourself to want. Hold to that vision. Now, having completed this course, you have not only cultivated awareness but have also established a structure, a rhythm, and a habit of return. You have learned to listen beneath the surface, to trust the deeper mind, the unconscious, as something that is not working against you, but speaking with you. Over time, it has instilled a quieter, steadier knowing. One you can trust. One that no longer needs to force or to prove. The call now is not to strive but to remain faithful. Now is not the time to live strictly in contemplation, but to hold the vision gently, stay aligned, and watch it be fulfilled.

Mod 12 // Day 1

Reading

When you arrive with an awareness of wholeness, something shifts. The constant seeking quiets. The drive to find something outside yourself settles. You no longer need to outsource your knowing or your fulfillment. A deeper peace takes root, softening the demands and impulses that once felt so loud. It's as if an inner hyperactivity has calmed. Like a child or puppy that settles with maturity, the nervous system no longer needs to thrash for reassurance. It's all energy. And with integration, that energy finds its rhythm. The trap is believing that peace or fulfillment will come from changing our circumstances. We look outward for answers, validation, or completion, assuming something is missing. **But wholeness doesn't arrive through external correction. It arrives through internal recognition.** When we turn inward, we stop seeing ourselves as the problem to be solved and begin to recognize that the solution has been within us all along.

This is why the story in *The Alchemist* by Paulo Coelho feels so mirrored in my own life. Santiago travels far in search of a treasure, only to discover it was waiting where he began. I had a similar realization after years of seeking mentors. I even traveled to England to meet with someone steeped in Jungian and alchemical wisdom. He was wise, and the trip was important to take. But it became clear, especially after returning, that I had been outsourcing my own authority. The wisdom I was seeking wasn't something another person could give me. It was something I needed to step into myself.

It took going all that way to England to see what had been true all along: the treasure was already within me. This is wholeness not the absence of challenge. But a settled knowing that you are not lacking, that you have access to what you need. If you find yourself searching for validation, direction, or proof, take a moment to pause. Come back to yourself. Ask gently: *What if I already have what I'm looking for?* The journey has mattered. Nothing has been wasted. But now, it's time to stop looking outside and begin living from the wholeness that has always been within you.

Journaling

What am I believing and experiencing today (emotionally, physically and spiritually)? What is my positive mindset and my negative mindset? How can I reparent myself with my current situation? What would the voice of Love say?

____

____

____

____

____

Vision

Reconnect to your Vision // What structure and implemenation needs to occur today?

____

____

Meditation

Dawnos *Reoriented* Album // Track 12 – Alchemy

Affirmation

Morning Affirmation _______________________________   Evening Affirmation _______________________________

Pausing (Write out the times // set alarms)

Morning _______________   Midday _______________   Afternoon _______________   Evening _______________

Physical Movement

Walking, Yoga, Running, Weight lifting, Stretching, Jiu Jitsu, Pilates, or another: _______________

Resistance (Tasks for the Day)

Creative ____

Professional ____

Relationship(s) ____

Self ____

Evening Review

How did it go? What lesson(s) did I learn? Who do I need to make an amends with or forgive?

____

____

Mod 12 // Day 2

Reading

Here's a truth that changes everything: what you are desiring is already here. You already have it. Not from a place of greed or ego-led neediness, but from a place of recognition. You are the light and the abundance. When you realize that you are the one you have been searching for, that you are whole, you are living in wholeness itself. From this place, you don't need anything outside of you. You're living in alignment. Think of those in their older years who have done the work—both the shadow work and the light work. They know they're okay with who they are. They're not chasing anything. And from this place of wholeness, they can give back freely because they don't need to impress or please anybody else. They're fulfilled, and they're doing what they want to do. But here's what's beautiful: in doing what they want to do, there's purpose, meaning, and love. They're not trying to "do anything". They're simply being themselves. And that place of being themselves, that energy, is what's healing those around them. They're not in their mind thinking, "I gotta do this" or "I gotta do that." It's natural, effortless, and authentic. And this natural way of being is the healing. It's what brings wholeness not just to them, but to everyone they encounter.

This is the paradox: when you stop searching for what you need, you discover you already have it. When you stop trying to become something, you realize you already are it. You are whole now. Not after you achieve something, fix yourself, or accumulate more. It is in this moment. So today, stop searching outside yourself, stop chasing and stop trying so hard. Instead, recognize what's already true: you are the light you've been seeking. You are the abundance you've been pursuing. You are the wholeness you've been longing for. Live from that place. Be from that place. And watch how your simple presence, your authentic being, becomes the very thing that heals and transforms everything around you. This is not something you do. It's who you are.

Journaling

What am I believing and experiencing today (emotionally, physically and spiritually)? What is my positive mindset and my negative mindset? How can I reparent myself with my current situation? What would the voice of Love say?

____

____

____

____

____

____

Vision

Reconnect to your Vision // What structure and implemenation needs to occur today?

____

____

Meditation

Dawnos _Air_ Album // Track 1 – Box Breath

Affirmation

Morning Affirmation _______________________   Evening Affirmation _______________________

Pausing   (Write out the times // set alarms)

Morning _____________   Midday _____________   Afternoon _____________   Evening _____________

Physical Movement

Walking, Yoga, Running, Weight lifting, Stretching, Jiu Jitsu, Pilates, or another: _______________

Resistance (Tasks for the Day)

Creative ____

Professional ____

Relationship(s) ____

Self ____

Evening Review

How did it go? What lesson(s) did I learn? Who do I need to make an amends with or forgive?

____

____

Mod 12 // Day 3

Reading

There is a helpful idea that encapsulates wholeness, drawn from a phrase by Neville Goddard: *live from the end*. At its core, this means that when we are living from wholeness, we are no longer operating from lack. We are not striving toward some future version of ourselves that will finally be enough; we are inhabiting the felt sense of completion now. Whatever feels absent or unresolved—financial strain, relational disconnection, estrangement, grief, sadness, or loss—is met not by reaching or grasping, but by embodying the larger self that already knows fulfillment. **Living from the end is not merely visualization; it is allowing yourself to fully feel what it would be like to be whole, connected, and at peace, here and now.**

This shifts the entire way we engage life. **When we live from the end, we are no longer moving from deficiency but with sufficiency.** There is an important distinction here. This is not egoic manifestation or an attempt to bend reality to personal gain. In fact, the way to test this practice is simple: does it arise from the mind of Love, and is it aligned with your deeper calling? Living from the end is not about getting more, it is about remembering what is already true. The moment we believe we are not whole, we slip into the ego's story of separation. But when we live as if it has already happened, we are not pretending or bypassing, we are returning to reality. We are not reaching for wholeness. We are already it.

> *"And the end of all our exploring*
> *will be to arrive where we started*
> *and know the place for the first time."* — T.S. Eliot from *Little Gidding*

Journaling

What am I believing and experiencing today (emotionally, physically and spiritually)? What is my positive mindset and my negative mindset? How can I reparent myself with my current situation? What would the voice of Love say?

____

____

____

____

____

____

Vision

Reconnect to your Vision // What structure and implemenation needs to occur today?

____

____

Meditation

Dawnos *Air* Album // Track 2 – Downshift

Affirmation

Morning Affirmation ___________________________   Evening Affirmation ___________________________________

Pausing   (Write out the times // set alarms)

Morning _____________   Midday _____________   Afternoon _____________   Evening _____________

Physical Movement

Walking, Yoga, Running, Weight lifting, Stretching, Jiu Jitsu, Pilates, or another: _______________

Resistance (Tasks for the Day)

Creative ____

Professional ____

Relationship(s) ____

Self ____

Evening Review

How did it go? What lesson(s) did I learn? Who do I need to make an amends with or forgive?

____

____

Mod 12 // Day 4

Reading

It's often said that **Carl Jung** possessed one of the largest personal libraries on alchemy in the world. Jung, one of the pioneers, or *fathers* if you will, of modern psychology, was deeply fascinated by alchemy not as a literal pursuit, but as a symbolic one. Incidentally, the root of the word *psyche* comes from the Greek, meaning *soul* or *breath*. From the beginning, psychology was concerned not just with the mind, but with the soul. Throughout history, alchemy has carried a kind of mythic allure, the secret art of turning lead into gold. Whether or not that ever happened in a literal sense is almost beside the point. What alchemy truly symbolizes, at least psychologically and spiritually, is a much deeper process: the transformation of pain into wisdom, wounds into meaning, and suffering into depth. In this sense, **alchemy is about taking what feels heavy—our pain, our wounds, our negative thoughts, emotions, and even bodily sensations—and allowing them to be transformed. Darkness becomes light. Hatred becomes love. Separation becomes connection. Smallness gives way to largeness.**

In *Iron John*, Robert Bly describes the masculine initiation as the place where "our wounds become our glory", or said another way, our gold. Similarly, Clarissa Pinkola Estés, in her book *Women Who Run with the Wolves*, speaks to the feminine initiation, carrying a parallel truth: our wounds are not a mistake, but a calling, an initiation into deeper life. Seen this way, **the work of therapy, the inner work, is not about fixing ourselves or making ourselves smaller, safer, or more acceptable. It is about giving ourselves fully to this initiation. It is about expansion.** About becoming large enough to be with whatever arises in our lives. When we stop fighting our pain, resisting it, or sending back more negativity, something shifts. We realize that *we* are the alchemical vessel. And through that process, forgiveness becomes possible. Love becomes possible. That is the gold.

Journaling

What am I believing and experiencing today (emotionally, physically and spiritually)? What is my positive mindset and my negative mindset? How can I reparent myself with my current situation? What would the voice of Love say?

Vision

Reconnect to your Vision // What structure and implemenation needs to occur today?

____

____

Meditation

Dawnos _Reoriented_ Album // Track 12 – Alchemy

Affirmation

Morning Affirmation _______________________________   Evening Affirmation _______________________________

Pausing   (Write out the times // set alarms)

Morning _____________   Midday _____________   Afternoon _____________   Evening _____________

Physical Movement

Walking, Yoga, Running, Weight lifting, Stretching, Jiu Jitsu, Pilates, or another: _______________

Resistance (Tasks for the Day)

Creative ____

Professional ____

Relationship(s) ____

Self ____

Evening Review

How did it go? What lesson(s) did I learn? Who do I need to make an amends with or forgive?

____

____

Reading

All of philosophy, spirituality, and psychology comes down to this most basic and fundamental statement: I am. When we sit, breathe, and meditate with simply "I am", it immediately seats us in the observing position, the witness. What I mean is this: **everything after *I am…* is usually a role, a story, a function we take on—often pulled from past and future, from illusion, from the thoughts and emotions we project. But I am, by itself, is a singular point of being, a place of soul, both a starting point and an end point.** As the scriptures say: the beginning and the end. It's the inner point of the circle.

So take a moment to pause and close your eyes. Let "I am" become an anchor—a single reference point, a grounding signal from which all energy flows, positive or negative. And from that place, you can begin to notice: am I moving from connection, truth, and love—or from separation, illusion, and fear? We always come back to I am. We can always come back to I am. It's simple and fundamental. And then we live from that place. It's pretty incredible when you think about it. It puts you back in charge, not in a controlling way but in a conscious way, returning you to what Gurdjieff might call the master's seat, the place where you can catch yourself.So instead of giving unnecessary power to *I am sad… I am mad… I am lonely… I am confused…* We stop, pause, notice, but we don't deny. We simply recognize: sadness is here… loneliness is here… without tying our identity to it. Then we return to I am.

And from there, the most courageous and healing practice becomes possible: I am loved. I am love. I am loving. And then: I am light. I am abundant. I am able. I am capable. I am whole. I am fulfilled. This practice can't help but change you. Right here, you stand at a threshold—two paths: light or dark, reality or illusion, heaven or hell, if you will. So take time. And be with I am.

Journaling

What am I believing and experiencing today (emotionally, physically and spiritually)? What is my positive mindset and my negative mindset? How can I reparent myself with my current situation? What would the voice of Love say?

____

____

____

____

____

____

Vision

Reconnect to your Vision // What structure and implemenation needs to occur today?

____

____

Meditation

Dawnos _Reoriented_ Album // Track 11 – I AM

Affirmation

Morning Affirmation _______________________________   Evening Affirmation _______________________________

Pausing   (Write out the times // set alarms)

Morning _____________   Midday _____________   Afternoon _____________   Evening _____________

Physical Movement

Walking, Yoga, Running, Weight lifting, Stretching, Jiu Jitsu, Pilates, or another: _______________

Resistance (Tasks for the Day)

Creative ____

Professional ____

Relationship(s) ____

Self ____

Evening Review

How did it go? What lesson(s) did I learn? Who do I need to make an amends with or forgive?

____

____

Reading

As we've already explored through the lens of alchemy, there is one essential truth worth naming clearly: we hold the power to choose how we co-create with Source. Whatever is given to us in our experience—negativity, pain, suffering, or difficulty—we are met with a fundamental choice. We can bring fear to it, or we can bring love. This choice is always there, though not always easy.

This idea of alchemy doesn't need to be complicated or abstract. It is profoundly practical. Here's what it looks like: You take the negative energy—your own, another's, or a situation itself—and instead of responding with fear, anger, or resentment, you choose to meet it with love and light. You hold it, sit with it, and then you let it go. This is the opposite of control. As I once heard in an Al-Anon meeting, the mother of all addiction is control. Alchemy is compassion in action, and it invites us into something far deeper: presence without grasping nor resisting. In this process, you hold the situation within yourself with greater capacity, with compassion rather than force. From that place, you bring your wholeness, your intention, your purpose. You are no longer trying to manage life, but participating in it. This is co-creation through devotion. You learn to hold people, circumstances, and outcomes loosely, with tenderness.

Another way to name this is compassion grounded in radical acceptance. It is the willingness to see reality as it is and to learn to love what *is*, not what you wish it to be. From that place, love is free to move, to direct its own course. And you are given the gift of participation in something sacred—a quiet, beautiful dance where fear loosens its grip, and love, promise, and compassion are allowed to lead.

Journaling

What am I believing and experiencing today (emotionally, physically and spiritually)? What is my positive mindset and my negative mindset? How can I reparent myself with my current situation? What would the voice of Love say?

____

____

____

____

____

____

____

Vision

Reconnect to your Vision // What structure and implemenation needs to occur today?

____

____

Meditation

Dawnos _Reoriented_ Album // Track 8 – Tonglen

Affirmation

Morning Affirmation ______________________________   Evening Affirmation ______________________________

Pausing   (Write out the times // set alarms)

Morning ______________   Midday ______________   Afternoon ______________   Evening ______________

Physical Movement

Walking, Yoga, Running, Weight lifting, Stretching, Jiu Jitsu, Pilates, or another: ______________

Resistance (Tasks for the Day)

Creative ____

Professional ____

Relationship(s) ____

Self ____

Evening Review

How did it go? What lesson(s) did I learn? Who do I need to make an amends with or forgive?

____

____

Mod 12 // Day 7

Reading

As these modules come to a close, my hope is that the daily practices themselves continue—that you've established a rhythm that no longer feels like a task or a chore, but a *get-to*, a *want-to*, something you genuinely look forward to. My hope is that you have made it your own, created a personal cadence, and come to see that just as your body loves movement, your soul loves these mental and spiritual exercises. It felt there was no more fitting way to close the final day of *The Holland Method* workbook than with the ultimate arrival: the present moment. Isn't that the true intention of all of this? **As Jesus said, *the kingdom of heaven is at hand*—right here, right now.**

So the final tool and practice is PRESENT. Bring to mind any situation, thought, or emotion that feels challenging, and use this tool as a way to gently practice and process whatever you're sitting with: P — Perceive. What are you perceiving? Is it coming from fear or from love? R — Reality. Is it actually true? Is it happening right now? E — Experience. Notice the body. Is there constriction, the ego body, or openness and lightness, the whole body? S — Source. Invite in help. Support beyond the smaller self. E — Explore. Become familiar with the felt sense of the experience. Stay curious. N — Nurture. Rather than resist, be with it. Allow the presence of the inner loving parent. T — Transform. Wait. Let the alchemy occur.

And here is the good news: no feeling is final, as Rilke reminds us. When you give yourself to a process like this, something truly does shift. A real transformation and alchemy take place. We discover that we can not only sit with ourselves in the present moment, but that we are co-creators within it. We find access to a peace that surpasses understanding. We realize we have the tools and practices to meet whatever arises, not to make us smaller, but to expand our capacity to love and to be of service. You are the miracle. You are the light of the world. And yours is a light that no one else can offer in quite the same way. The world needs each of us to bring forth this PRESENT—this gift of presence—this heaven on earth, offered again to those who have forgotten.

Journaling

What am I believing and experiencing today (emotionally, physically and spiritually)? What is my positive mindset and my negative mindset? How can I reparent myself with my current situation? What would the voice of Love say?

____

____

____

____

____

____

Vision

Reconnect to your Vision // What structure and implemenation needs to occur today?

____

____

Meditation

Dawnos *Reoriented* Album // Track 10 – PRESENT

Affirmation

Morning Affirmation _______________________________   Evening Affirmation _______________________________

Pausing   (Write out the times // set alarms)

Morning _____________   Midday _____________   Afternoon _____________   Evening _____________

Physical Movement

Walking, Yoga, Running, Weight lifting, Stretching, Jiu Jitsu, Pilates, or another: _______________

Resistance (Tasks for the Day)

Creative ____

Professional ____

Relationship(s) ____

Self ____

Evening Review

How did it go? What lesson(s) did I learn? Who do I need to make an amends with or forgive?

____

____

Notes:

Appendix: Practices

Affirmations

Being (Ground & Identity)	Capacity (Inner Strength)	Trust (Release & Direction)	Love (Connection & Return)
I am loved.	I can listen to the voice of Love.	I can trust myself.	Love is with me.
I am whole.	I can sit with my emotions.	I can trust this vision.	I am held.
I am enough.	I can feel without reacting.	I don't have to have all the answers.	I can return to love.
I am worthy.	I can be present.	I can take this one day at a time.	I am forgiven.
I am safe.	I can slow down.	I can release control.	I am not alone.
I am good.	I am capable.	I can let this unfold.	I belong.
I like who I am.	I am strong.	I am guided.	I am supported.
I am here.	I can handle this.	I am moving in the right direction.	There is a light in me.
Nothing is wrong with me.	I am creative.	I can follow what feels true.	I carry light.
I am becoming more myself.	I am abundant.	I can let go.	I can forgive.

Breathwork –

Dawnos "Air" Album

Air is a collection of breathwork practices designed to support *The Work*—the daily rhythm of grounding, presence, and intentional living. These practices use the breath as a direct pathway into the body and nervous system, helping you regulate, reset, and reconnect throughout the day. Rather than forcing calm or chasing altered states, Air invites you to work with breath in a simple, accessible way—meeting the body where it is and allowing it to lead. Through practices that balance, energize, expand, and slow the system, breath becomes a steady companion: something you return to when you feel scattered, overwhelmed, or disconnected. Air reminds you that the breath is always available, offering a reliable way back into presence, clarity, and inner steadiness.

Track 1 // Box Breath – a focused breath practice that uses equal counts to establish rhythm and stability in the body. By tracing a simple four-part pattern, the breath helps calm the nervous system and bring the mind into a steady and balanced present state.

Track 2 // Downshift – a calming breathing practice that intentionally lengthens the exhale to signal safety to the nervous system. By using a gentle imbalance—longer exhale than inhale—the body naturally settles out of alertness and into regulation.

Track 3 // Fire Breath – an energizing breath practice designed to wake up the system that uses rhythmic, belly-driven breathing to build heat, clarity, and focus, followed by breath holds that allow the body to integrate and stabilize the energy created.

Track 4 // Expansion Breath – a breathing practice that invites the body to expand creating room naturally through the diaphragm, ribs, and lungs. Without counts or force, it helps cultivate spaciousness, ease, and a deeper sense of embodiment.

Track 5 // Space – focuses on the natural gaps between breaths rather than the breath itself. This practice encourages rest, presence, and a soft release of control by allowing awareness to settle into the space in between.

Track 6 // Rhythm Breath – invites the body into a steady, circular cadence—allowing energy to circulate, settle, and come into coherence. Through gentle nose breathing, the system finds a felt sense of balance, aliveness, and calm clarity.

Available on all major streaming platforms.

Guided Meditations // Visualizations

Dawnos "Oriented" Album

(Modules 1-4)

Oriented is about establishing inner ground. These meditations support you in settling your nervous system, quieting the mind, and remembering who you are beneath the constant movement of life. The practices invite you into vision, breath, presence, and connection—helping you orient inward before engaging deeper emotional or psychological work. Through images of the ocean, sacred space, light, and the body's felt sense, you are guided back into steadiness and clarity. Oriented is an invitation to come home to yourself, reconnect with Source, and establish a stable inner foundation from which intention, trust, and meaning can naturally arise.

Dawnos "Disoriented" Album

(Modules 5-8)

Disoriented brings you into the honest terrain of inner disruption—the places where old patterns, emotions, and beliefs begin to surface. These meditations support you in meeting fear, grief, confusion, and internal conflict with compassion rather than avoidance. Through practices of self-inquiry, emotional awareness, and parts work, you are guided to expand your capacity to stay present with what is difficult without becoming overwhelmed. Disoriented reframes confusion not as failure, but as a meaningful threshold—a necessary stage of growth where deeper understanding, emotional strength, and self-compassion begin to take root.

Dawnos "Reoriented" Album

(Modules 9-12)

Reoriented marks a movement into integration, surrender, and a larger way of being. These meditations invite you to release control, soften into the unknown, and allow transformation to unfold in its own time. Through practices centered on presence, gratitude, compassion, and alchemy, you are guided from effort into flow, from fear into trust, and from fragmentation into wholeness. Reoriented is not about fixing yourself, but about living from a deeper center—where shadow and light are held together, powerlessness becomes wisdom, and love becomes the orientation from which you live.

Available on all major streaming platforms.

Appendix: Tools

THE WORK

A DAILY RHYTHM AND PRACTICE

VISION
(Morning)

ALIGNING YOUR LIFE WITH WHAT TRULY MATTERS TO YOUR SOUL.

JOURNALING

LISTENING TO YOUR INNER WORLD AND GIVING IT A VOICE.

AFFIRMATION

REORIENTING YOUR MIND TOWARD LOVE, WORTH, AND POSSIBILITY.

MEDITATION

RETURNING TO PRESENCE BY QUIETING THE MIND AND LISTENING WITHIN.

READING

REORIENTATING TO TRUTH, OFFERING INSPIRATION AND ALIGNMENT WITH WHO YOU ARE AND WHERE YOU'RE GOING

PAUSING

STEPPING OUT OF AUTOPILOT TO RECONNECT WITH YOUR PURPOSE.

RESISTANCE

FACING THE PLACES WE AVOID - AND MOVING THROUGH IT UNLOCKING ENERGY AND CLARITY.

PHYSICAL MOVEMENT

SHIFTING YOUR PHYSICAL STATE, TO RESTORE YOUR EMOTIONAL BALANCE.

VISION
(Evening)

REVIEWING THE DAY - SPACE FOR REFLECTION AND ALIGNMENT BEFORE REST.

THE VISION

LIVING OUT YOUR PURPOSE

COMMIT TO ACTION
(DAILY TASKS)
FACE THE OBSTACLES
ESTABLISH A STRUCTURE
IDENTIFY YOUR GIFTS
CLARIFY YOUR CALL
VISION

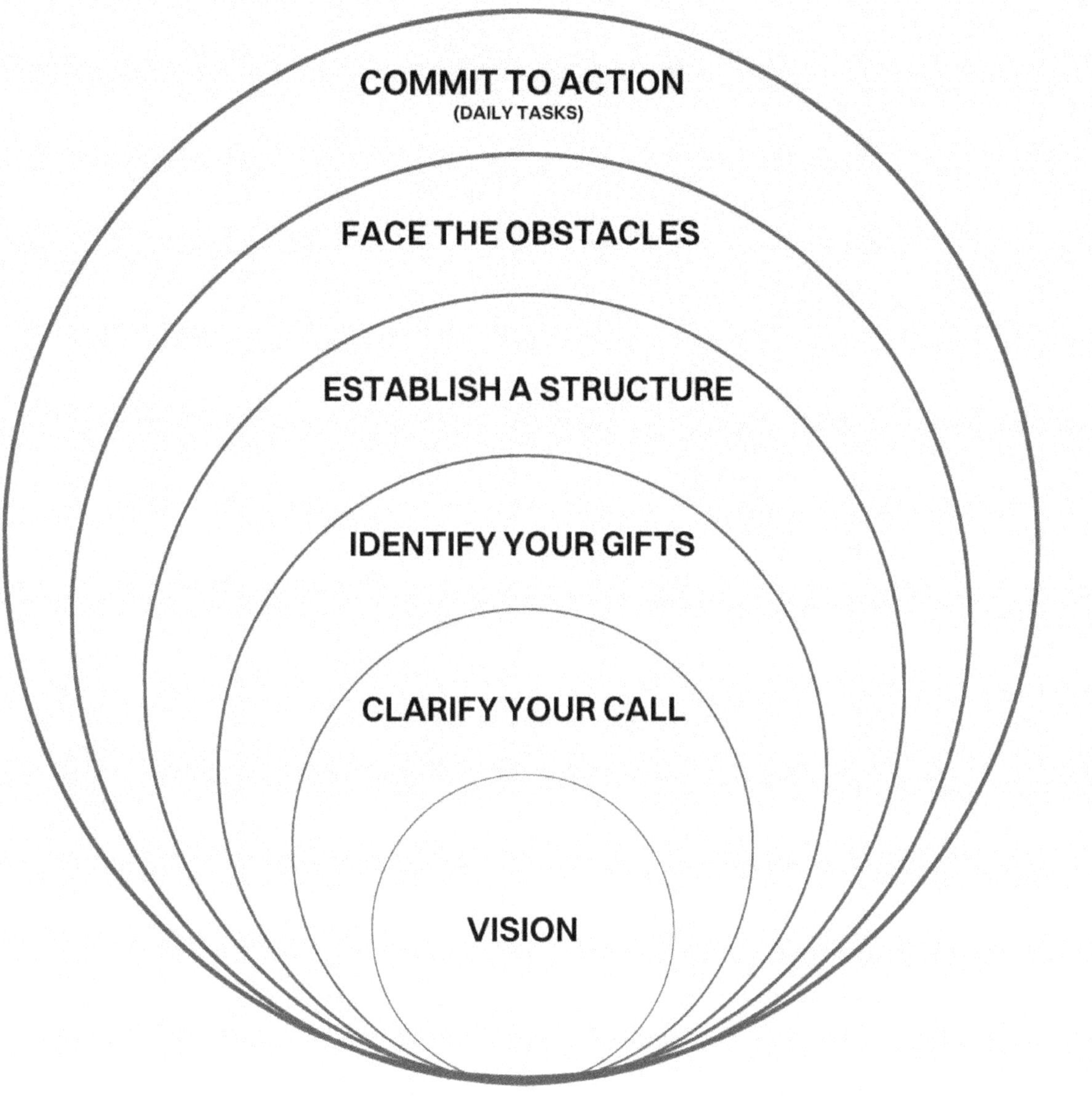

THE SHADOW

THREE LENSES THAT BLOCK SEEING CLEARLY

TRAUMA MODEL
TRUE SELF
PATTERNS MODEL
STORY MODEL

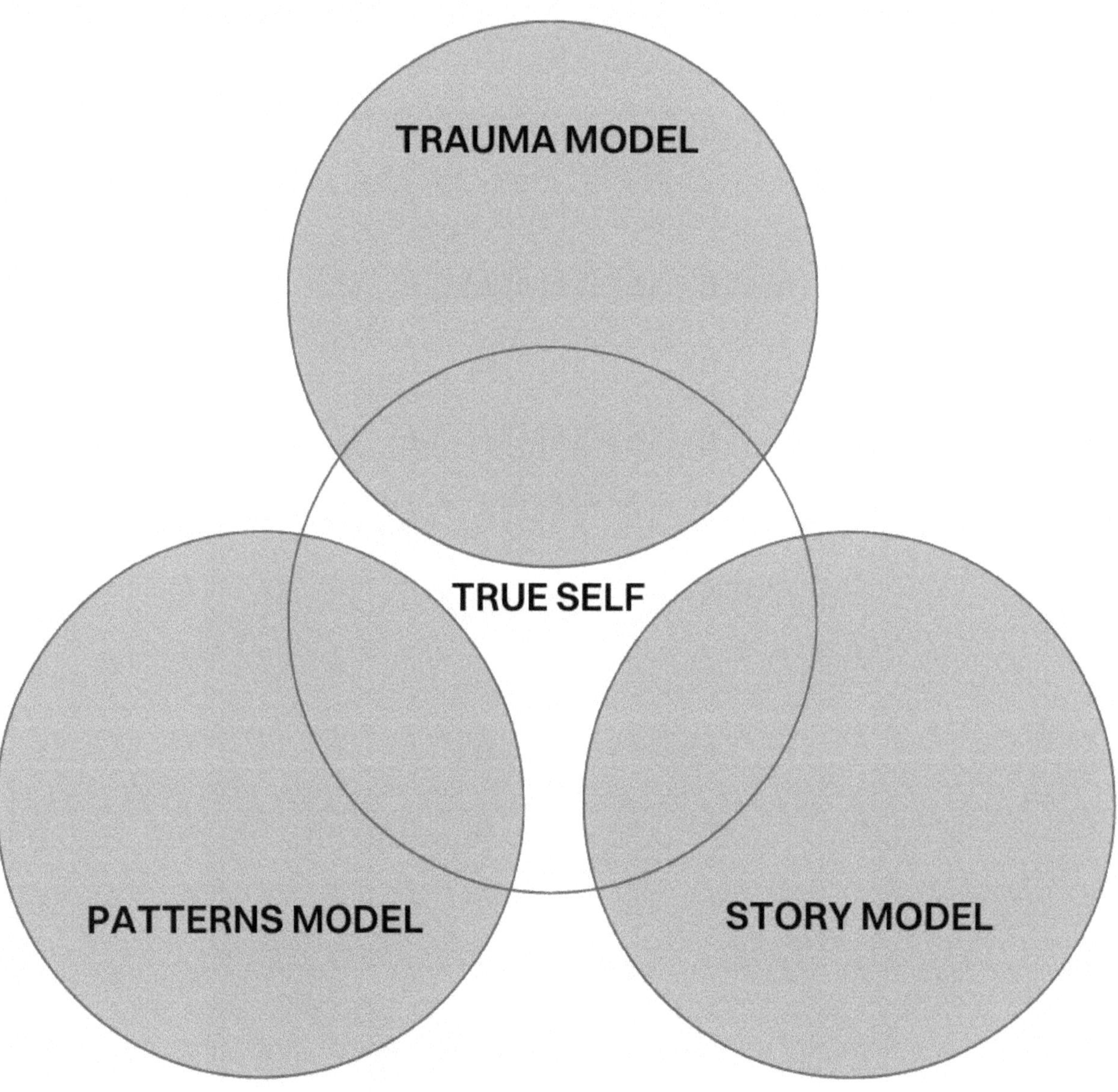

SOURCE

A TOOL TO AID IN ACCESSING A POWER GREATER THAN YOURSELF

SEEK — Invite a Higher Power, whether you call it God or define it as your Source, to be present with you in this moment.

OPEN — Stay open to hearing, observing, and listening for that Source. Be mindful of anything that may be hindering your connection.

UNKNOWN — Embrace the unknown found in silence and observation, allowing yourself to acknowledge any distractions that draw you away from this space.

RESOURCE — Reach out to anyone or anything that has influenced your life—mentors, teachers, family, even those who are no longer with us. If you're seeking wisdom, welcome it into your life.

COMPASSION — Embrace receiving compassion and support from those who have come to mind.

EXPERIENCE — Embrace this moment fully; take note of the qualities, thoughts, and emotions that arise within you right now.

FELT SENSE

A PRACTICE TO CONNECT TO THE BODY MORE DEEPLY

1 LOCATION — If the energy were located in the body, where would it be? Notice where your body is uncomfortable. Typically, it is the first place that comes to mind.

2 COLOR — Colors can represent energy. Connecting to colors it allows you to connect more to the energy. This is also part of Chakra work, which has been around for thousands of years and is represented by colors.

3 SHAPE | SYMBOL — Identifying a shape/symbol accesses a different part of the brain region.

4 WEIGHT — There is often a weight and heaviness to our ego body's pain. How heavy does it feel?

5 TEMPERATURE — Energy has a temperature to it. We will often feel hot, warm, or cold. Often it is related to different emotions. For example, anger is often heat whereas fear, shame, or loneliness is cold.

6 AGE — This question helps make a connection to older energy of the past most often of childhood that has been stored.

THE QUESTIONS

A TOOL TO HELP YOU CHANGE THE WAY YOU THINK ABOUT YOUR CIRCUMSTANCES

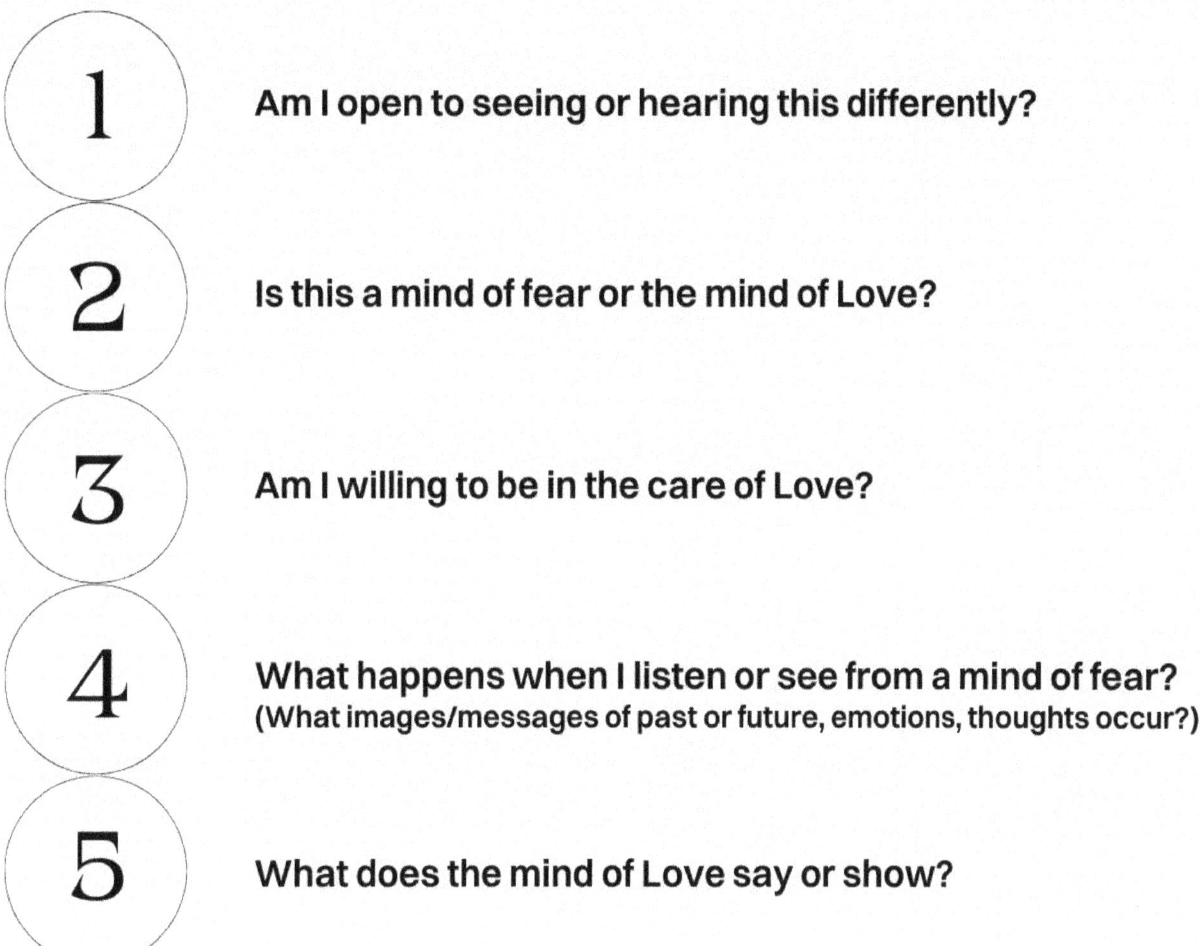

1 — Am I open to seeing or hearing this differently?

2 — Is this a mind of fear or the mind of Love?

3 — Am I willing to be in the care of Love?

4 — What happens when I listen or see from a mind of fear?
(What images/messages of past or future, emotions, thoughts occur?)

5 — What does the mind of Love say or show?

EMOTIONAL CYCLE

EMOTIONAL INFLAMMATION, COMPLETING THE EMOTIONAL CYCLE

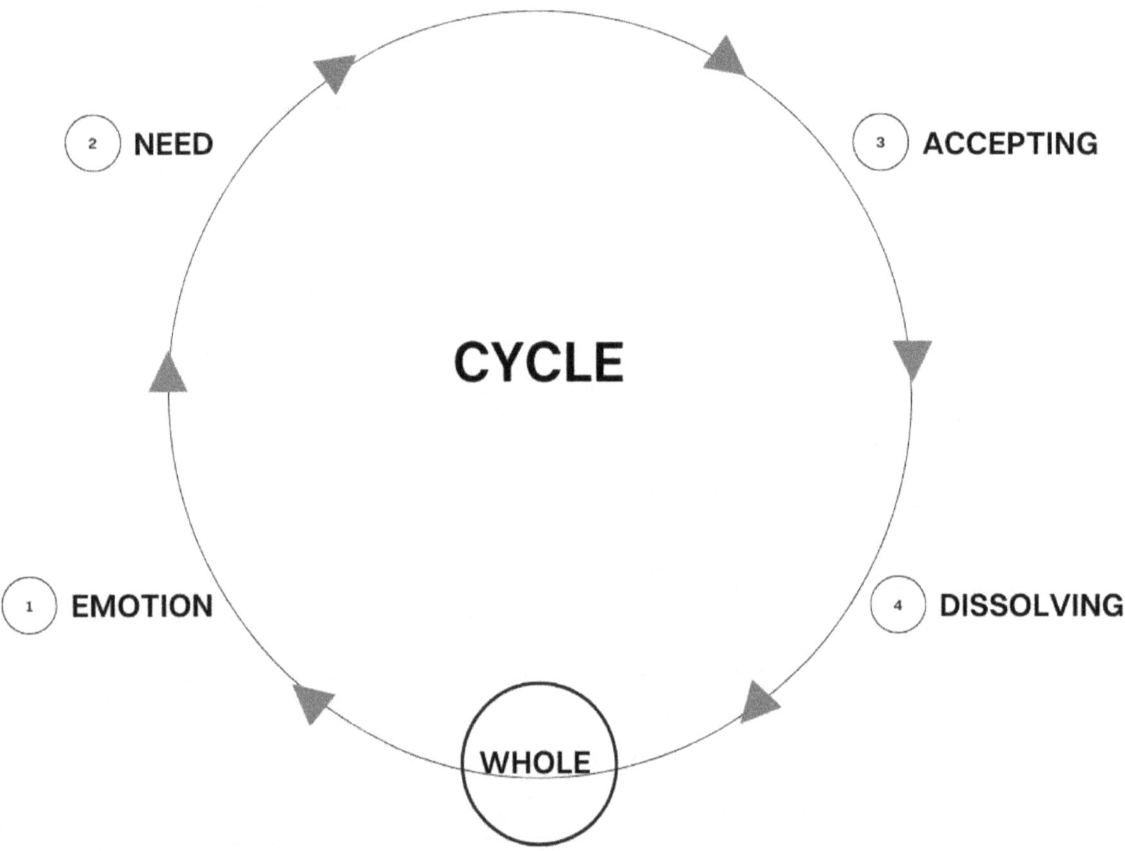

PARENT

A TOOL TO HELP REPARENT YOURSELF AND INTEGRATE SPLIT PARTS OF YOU BACK TO SELF

P — PART — Identify the part of you that is feeling distress, the emotions, the thoughts, etc.

A — ASK — Access/Ask/Analyze where you are feeling it in your body. Allow yourself to fully connect to this part of you.

R — REMEMBER — Remember a moment from your childhood and reflect on everything you experienced—particularly what was left unfinished and what you needed but didn't receive. Visualize yourself in that situation. Connect with that younger version of yourself as deeply as you can. Concentrate on a vivid picture of yourself during that period in your life.

E — ENVISION — Envision a perfect childhood environment, a space that would have been ideally tailored for you. Envision nurturing and loving parental figures, paying attention to the details, traits, and qualities you needed during that time. Have fun with it for a moment!

N — NURTURE — Notice these loving parental qualities being shown to you. Notice being fully nurtured especially through the troubling parts of you that have been painful. Then see your adult self nurturing this part of you.

T — TRANSFORM — Wait for an Alchemy to occur. This energy will dissolve. The intensity will lessen.

VORTEX

IN THE VORTEX OF CHAOS, A HIDDEN ORDER EMERGES

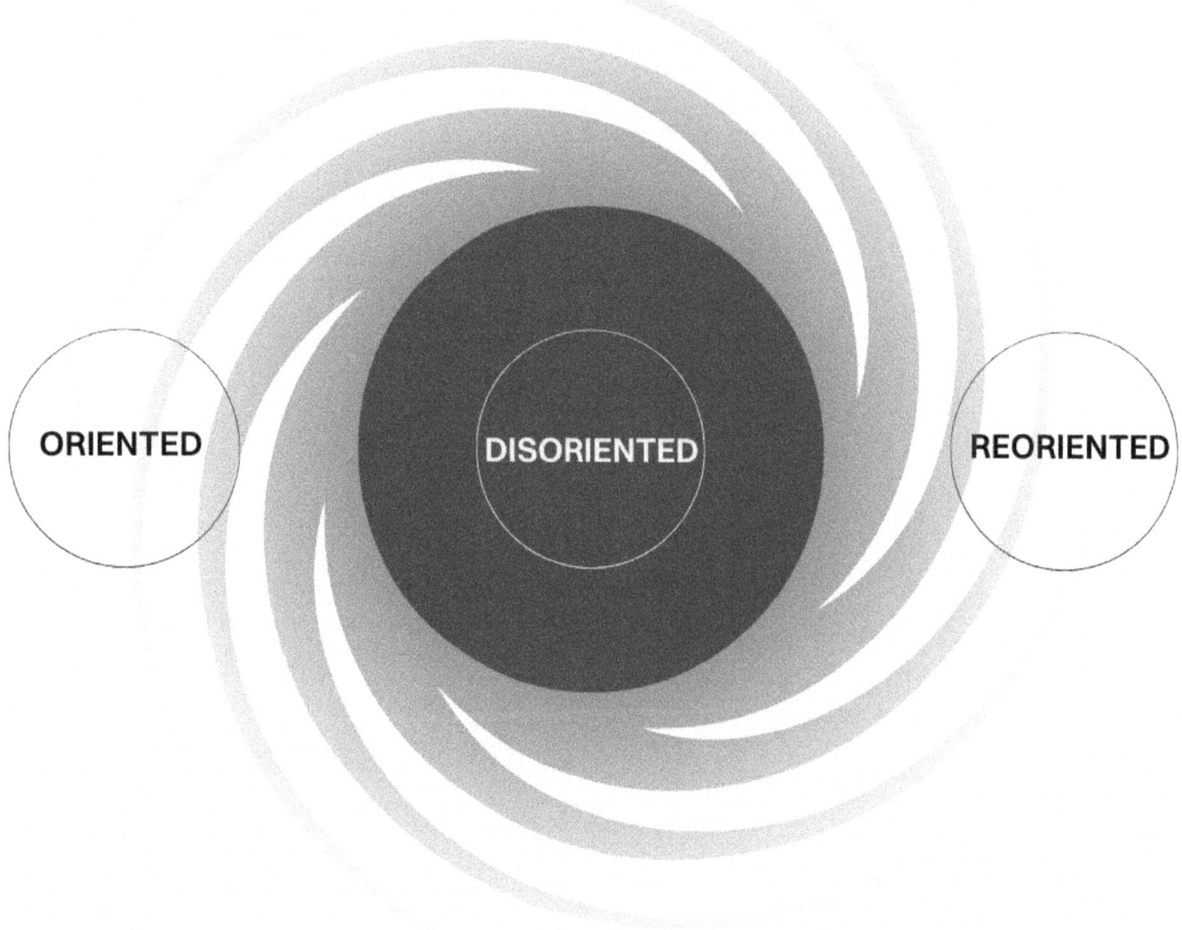

OPEN

A TOOL TO HELP CONNECT TO THE NEGATIVE ENERGY AND STATE IN ORDER TO SHIFT

O — **OBSERVE IT** — Feel the emotions, notice the thoughts, and the story you are thinking and believing.

P — **PERMISSION** — Rather than resist the energy, try to allow it to be here, engage it.

E — **EXPLORE** — Inquire the following in the body: Location, Shape, Weight, Color, Temperature, Age (younger self).

N — **NURTURE** — Allow yourself to merge with the energy, become one with it, nurture yourself through it.

HOPE

A TOOL TO RECONNECT TO INNER STRENGTH BY HONORING YOUR EXPERIENCE AND OPENING TO POSSIBILITY.

H — **HUMANITY**

This involves fully embracing the entirety of our thoughts, emotions, and feelings. It is about experiencing the richness of life and allowing ourselves to fully engage in every moment.

O — **OPEN**

The pivot involves embracing the vastness and expansiveness that lies beyond oneself. It means opening yourself to the broader world that exists beyond your individual perspective and experience.

P — **PEACE**

With this shift, you embrace the notion of "it is as it should be," and a profound sense of peace begins to emerge.

E — **EVERYTHING**

At this ultimate juncture, the understanding that you are intertwined with everything, and that everything is intertwined with you, becomes a profound realization.

THIRDWAY

1 FIGHT | CLINGING

Clinging or escalating often springs from anger and fear—the shadow of control that tries to force solutions from a power stance, reducing everything to right vs. wrong.

2 FLIGHT | ADVERSION

When fear drives avoidance, we exercise control by not engaging—momentary relief that only postpones the real work.

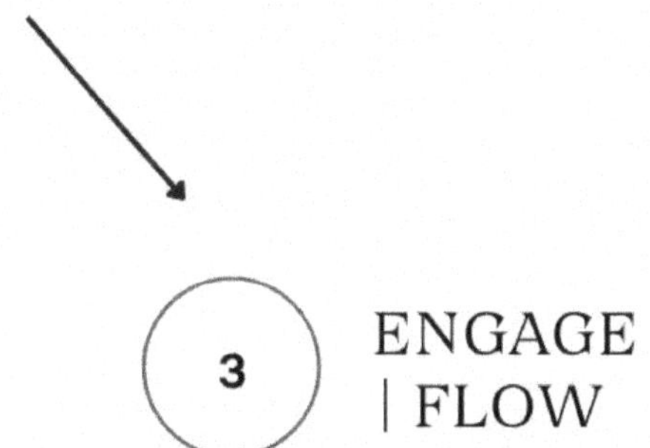

3 ENGAGE | FLOW

The third way receives the energy and softens it into peace and connection, releasing the demand for an immediate fix. From this stance—"everything is as it should be"—we let events unfold for ourselves and others, meeting what comes and working with it.

PRESENT

A TOOL INTEGRATING THE FULL RANGE OF THE HEALING PROCESS

P — **PERCEIVE** — Notice how you are seeing a troubling situation. Are you perceiving from a state of fear?

R — **REALITY** — Question if your perception is Reality. Is it true?

E — **EXPERIENCE** — Noticing how your Body is responding. Is it from the Ego's Body's perspective or Whole Body?

S — **SOURCE** — Invite in Help. Bring in Love, Support, Truth, and Peace.

E — **EXPLORE** — Become familiar with the Felt Sense of the energy you are holding.

N — **NURTURE** — Rather than resist the energy, try to allow it to be here, engage it. Nurture by merging with the energy. Learn to not resist it.

T — **TRANSFORM** — Wait for an Alchemy to occur. This energy will dissolve. The intensity will lessen.

LEAP

A TOOL FOR DISCERNMENT AND TRUSTING YOUR INNER VOICE

L — **LOVE** — Is this coming from love rather than fear? Does it move you toward connection instead of self-protection?

E — **EXPANSION** — Does this open you into greater freedom and growth? Or does it contract you into old patterns?

A — **ALIVENESS** — Does this bring energy, vitality, and presence into your body? Or does it drain and diminish you?

P — **PURPOSE** — Does this align with your deeper calling? Does it serve something larger than your ego?

Appendix: Resource List

The Holland Method has been shaped by contemplative spirituality, depth psychology, creativity practice, and embodied awareness. The following works have significantly influenced the development of this framework and are recommended for those who wish to explore more deeply.

Richard Rohr — Falling Upward

A profound exploration of the "two halves of life." Rohr reframes failure, loss, and disorientation as necessary initiations into deeper wisdom and spiritual maturity.

Richard Rohr — Breathing Underwater

A contemplative interpretation of the Twelve Steps. Rohr expands the idea of addiction beyond substances to the human tendency toward control, offering a path of surrender and awakening.

James Finley — The Healing Path

Blending contemplative Christianity with psychological insight, Finley gently guides readers into healing trauma and awakening to their deeper identity beyond wounded conditioning.

Robert Bly — Iron John

A mythopoetic exploration of masculine initiation and psychological maturation. Through story and archetype, Bly illuminates the journey from immaturity to grounded adulthood.

Julia Cameron — The Artist's Way

A spiritually rooted guide to reclaiming creativity. Cameron's emphasis on daily practice, rhythm, and inner listening deeply resonates with the training structure of The Holland Method.

Marianne Williamson — A Return to Love

A powerful invitation to shift from fear to love. Williamson reframes perception as the foundation of healing and transformation.

Marianne Williamson — Mystic Jesus

An exploration of the mystical heart of Christian teaching, calling readers beyond dogma into lived, embodied love.

Byron Katie — Loving What Is

A practical method for examining stressful thoughts. Katie's inquiry process mirrors the cognitive and awareness practices woven throughout The Holland Method.

Thich Nhat Hanh — You Are Here

A gentle and accessible introduction to mindful presence. Nhat Hanh reminds us that peace is not somewhere else — it is available in this breath.

Gordon Peerman — The Body Knows the Way

An invitation to trust embodied wisdom. Peerman emphasizes that healing unfolds not through force, but through listening.

Gordon Peerman — Blessed Relief

A compassionate exploration of surrender and spiritual release, guiding readers toward rest in what is already present.

Parker J. Palmer — Let Your Life Speak

A reflection on vocation as something discovered through listening rather than striving. Palmer invites readers to honor both their gifts and their wounds as guides toward authentic calling.

David Whyte — Consolations

A poetic meditation on essential human words such as courage, grief, and love. Whyte's reflections deepen the interior language needed for authentic living.

Rick Rubin — The Creative Act: A Way of Being

A reflection on creativity as a spiritual posture. Rubin articulates creativity not as performance, but as attentiveness and receptivity — a theme woven throughout this work.

Rickson Gracie — Breathe

A memoir of discipline, resilience, and embodied mastery. Gracie's reflections on breath, composure under pressure, and the integration of strength and surrender mirror the grounded, interior work central to this method.

Clarissa Pinkola Estés — Women Who Run with the Wolves

A Jungian exploration of the wild feminine psyche through myth and story. Estés invites readers to recover instinct, intuition, and the deep interior knowing that precedes cultural conditioning.

Adult Children of Alcoholics / Dysfunctional Families — The ACA Yellow Workbook

A structured recovery guide for healing the effects of family dysfunction. Its emphasis on inner child work, reparenting, emotional regulation, and daily practice has deeply informed the relational and integration components of this method.

Anthony de Mello — The Way to Love

A concise and piercing invitation into awareness. De Mello challenges attachment, illusion, and ego-driven perception, guiding readers toward freedom through radical clarity and awakened love.

Parker J. Palmer — Let Your Life Speak

A reflection on vocation as something discovered through listening rather than striving. Palmer invites readers to honor both their gifts and their wounds as guides toward authentic calling.

Rich Roll — Finding Ultra

A memoir of recovery, endurance, and radical reinvention. Roll's journey from addiction to ultra-endurance athlete embodies discipline, surrender, and the long arc of transformation through daily commitment.

Wendell Berry — Jayber Crow

A contemplative novel of belonging and quiet faithfulness. Through Jayber's life, Berry explores rootedness, unrequited love, humility, and the sacredness of place — inviting readers into a slower, steadier way of being.

A Course in Miracles

A spiritual text centered on the transformation of perception from fear to love. It teaches that peace is not found by changing the world, but by changing the mind through forgiveness and awareness.

Podcasts & Recorded Conversations

In addition to written works, the following recorded conversations have influenced the development of *The Holland Method*. These dialogues explore neuroscience, contemplative awareness, creativity, and interior stillness.

Andrew Huberman — Neuroscience & Self-Regulation

Selected episode exploring nervous system regulation, attention, and behavioral change. Huberman's integration of science and practice informs the breathwork and embodied awareness components of this method.

Tetragrammaton with Rick Rubin — Conversation with Jon Kabat-Zinn

A contemplative dialogue on mindfulness, awareness, and the discipline of presence. This conversation bridges creativity and meditation in a way that deeply resonates with the architecture of this work.

Recorded Video

Richard Rohr — "Becoming Stillness"

A recorded teaching on contemplative surrender and the movement into interior stillness.

Gerry Lopez — The Yin & Yang of Gerry Lopez

A portrait of legendary surfer Gerry Lopez, embodying flow, discipline, humility, and harmony with nature. The documentary reflects the balance of strength and surrender central to this work.

Rick Rubin — Shangri-La

A documentary series exploring creativity as a spiritual practice. Rubin's approach emphasizes stillness, receptivity, and the removal of ego from the artistic process.

Buck Brannaman — Buck

A documentary following horse trainer Buck Brannaman, whose work reflects quiet leadership, emotional regulation, and attuned presence. The film embodies strength without force and discipline without aggression.

Wendell Berry — Look & See: A Portrait of Wendell Berry

A contemplative documentary exploring Berry's life, land ethic, and commitment to rootedness. The film reinforces themes of place, stewardship, and the sacred rhythm of ordinary life.

Ram Dass — Ram Dass, Going Home

A contemplative documentary filmed near the end of Ram Dass's life. Through reflections on death, service, and surrender, the film invites a gentle acceptance of impermanence and a softening into presence.